the
Savvy Girl's
MONEY BOOK

This book is lovingly dedicated to the memory of my mother, Adele.

EMILY CHANTIRI

the
Savvy Girl's
MONEY BOOK

the savvy way to have the life you want

£75

CONTENTS

CHAPTER ONE

THE CINDERELLA CONSPIRACY

Once upon a time there was a beautiful girl named Penelope. She lived in a penthouse overlooking a sparkling harbour. In between manicures and lunch dates with her girlfriends, Penelope loved nothing more than to shop.

And why not? Her handsome, loving and rich husband, Robert, got just as much pleasure watching his wife max out her platinum card each month as she did spending the money. After all, the card was a gift from him for their first wedding anniversary.

The couple surrounded themselves with the latest clothes, fashion accessories, cars, boats and trips to exclusive islands that the other half just dream about...

Stop right there.

This is where the fairytale ends and the reality sinks in. If your life is anything like Penelope and Robert's then this book is not for you. This book is for the rest of us, the millions of working women earning a living and trying to make ends meet.

We work hard and we love life. We juggle our time with friends, family, jobs and (if we're good that week) gym. We love coffee dates with our girlfriends, chatting about our latest romance — or lack of romance.

We're doing pretty well, and we need to, because there is no rich Prince Charming around the next corner.

Fairytales like the one above do come true — just often enough to keep the women's magazines in cover stories. Sure, Aussie girl Mary Donaldson met a real prince and now she's Crown Princess Mary of Denmark. But that's one prince between about 10.3 million women. With nearly 30 million of us in the UK, even if maths isn't your strong point, you'll agree that these are fairly hopeless odds.

Leaving princes out of it, you are very, very unlikely to find someone who wants to keep you without you lifting a finger. (And if you should happen to, how long will it last till he sets his sights on trophy wife number two?) No, these days we want our own careers and our own money. It's the difference between being independent like Carrie in 'Sex and the City' or being handcuffed to someone else's money, like Gabrielle in 'Desperate Housewives'.

Whether we're single or not, childless or not, we need our own incomes in order to have the lives we want.

Sure it's possible for most couples to live permanently on one wage. You just can't live in a capital city, you sure can't buy a home, you can't travel, you'll be shopping at Primark, and you'll be asking yourself if you really need to buy meat more than once a fortnight.

And even if you're footloose and fancy-free there are plenty of everyday expenses. A working girl needs a working wardrobe, including hair, shoes, cosmetics and accessories, all of which require frequent updating. Then there are out-of-work activities: more clothes, drinks and meals out, movies, petrol, weekends away with the gang. And we haven't even mentioned rent, groceries or phone bills yet. It is very expensive being you!

But it doesn't need to be so pricey that you can barely keep your head above water. You'll be surprised how a few savvy tricks can change your lifestyle now, your future dreams and the way you feel about yourself.

I know it's a bit eye-glazing to even have to think about money, let alone sit down to plough your way through a superannuation statement. Don't worry, I understand that time is precious and attention is short. Trust me, if I ever forget, my sisters will remind me of that.

I wasn't born financially savvy. I had to learn, too. For me it started a few years ago with a book club. Each month I'd get together with a group of friends, have a wonderful meal, nice wine and a chat about books, life and love. We were a mixed bunch — some had families, some were single, some were high flyers, others were just starting out. But we had one thing in common and we spotted it fairly quickly: none of us were money smart. Even the ones who were in executive jobs, running big corporate budgets! In fact I was the only one who had any investments at all, owning some shares.

But we all wished we felt more in control of things. So we revved each other up and decided to do something about it. We turned the book club into an investment club. We learned it all from scratch, and we did it together. It was great, and we were soon making money.

In fact we did so well that I suggested we write our story. Four of us did and the book, *The Money Club*, became a bestseller. Three years later we followed up with another success, *Financially Fit for Life*.

So, there I am, with two books under my belt and lots of strangers telling me how useful the advice had been and how it had changed their lives. But it was a different story in my own family. I'm one of five sisters (yes, the bathroom fights were shockers when we were growing up). Two of my sisters didn't need any help; they were already on the way to money smarts. But my other two sisters definitely needed a hand. They had good jobs and they were intelligent, but they found money boring to think about and embarrassing to talk about. So every month they found themselves down to their last penny.

Easy enough to fix, right? They just needed to take my advice direct from the books. I gave them each a copy. The reaction was the same. 'Sure, I'll get round to it.' Meaning: much as I love you, not in this lifetime.

Here's my sister Rhonda's take on what happened:

I can honestly say I was over the moon for Emily. I was telling everyone that my sister had written a book. But time really is an issue for me. I know everybody says that, but I start work at 8 am and don't finish till late. At the end of the day I just want to go to bed. I'll buy a magazine and sometimes it will sit on the shelf for three weeks before I read it.

I just wish I'd read Em's books sooner.

In the past I was used to being in relationships where I had no commitment. And when you don't have commitment you are independent and you do things for yourself. I was with my previous boyfriend for four years and we had separate bank accounts. It became obvious we were not going to stay together when he bought one investment flat on his own, then another. He did not involve me in the whole process. Maybe I was too independent! Anyway we separated and I was single again.

I started going out, started partying and started spending. I was spending money on new shoes, clothes, clubs, cafes, food, drinks and the rest. I have always worked hard, but soon I was working weekends to make ends meet.

Now I'm in a committed relationship and recently we got married. Three-and-a-half years into this relationship, we opened a savings account together. This was the first time I had to share my money. I was so used to having my money for myself.

We opened the account together because we were going to buy property.

I started to take my finances seriously, even buying a software package to do a 'proper budget'.

But those first two books of Emily's are still under my bed, gathering dust.

(Don't you just love her honesty!)

I always thought to myself I should pull them out and read them and learn something, but still I didn't do it. But then she decided to write this book, for girls like me. I was her guinea-pig and now here I am, after all these years of being clueless about money, having saved for my wedding and to my astonishment, my husband and I have just bought a home together. It's amazing how much difference it has made to understand about money at last, and to be able to use it to get where I want to be. **Rhonda, 34**

Rhonda helped me, too. By using her as my guinea-pig, I figured out just what kind of help a girl who thought she could *never* get her head around money issues needed. Now she's so money savvy I just stand back and watch her go! If Rhonda did it, you can too.

CHAPTER TWO

SO WHERE DOES ALL MY MONEY GO?

The best way to understand where all your money goes is to break down a typical day in your life. We are going to start off with the little items first. Your daily expenses may look something like Sally's, who is about to get a real wake-up call.

Sally is 31, single and works for a firm of architects. After a big weekend – too many cocktails on Friday and Saturday night and a movie on Sunday – Sally thinks to herself, 'Thank goodness it's Monday, I can give my wallet a rest.'

Let's have a look at a typical Monday for Sally.

8.00 am	Weekly travel ticket	£10.00
8.30 am	She grabs a coffee and toast and heads into the office.	£3.00
9.00 am	Her favourite magazine has hit the newsstands.	£3.00
11.00 am	Someone in the office is going out for coffees, they take orders for everyone.	£1.50
1.00 pm	Lunch (meal and a drink)	£4.50
6.00 pm	After that busy weekend there's nothing in the fridge for dinner. She buys Thai take-away.	£8.00
	TOTAL	**£30.00**

Then Tuesday. Travel expenses and magazines are not on the agenda, so her daily expenses should be a lot cheaper, right? Unfortunately, not.

8.30 am	She grabs a coffee and toast and heads into the office.	£3.00
11.00 am	Someone in the office is going out for coffees.	£1.50
1.00 pm	Lunch	£4.50
7.00 pm	Tuesday night movie deal and a quick bite to eat with a friend. Last night Sally stayed home. Tonight she needs to get out.	£17.50
	TOTAL	**£26.50**

Are things looking any better for Wednesday? Afraid not.

7.30 am	Shared personal trainer	£20.00
8.30 am	She grabs a coffee and toast and heads into the office.	£3.00
11.00 am	Someone in the office is going out for coffees.	£1.50
1.00 pm	Lunch	£4.50
	TOTAL	**£29.00**

As the week progresses, Sally's expenses continue. Thursday's expenses will look no different from the other days. Friday will be a killer on the wallet as she starts the day again with her trainer and then in the evening goes out with her girlfriends. It's fair to say her expenses for Friday will be double the other days.

Now let's see how Sally's costs are broken up for the week.

Before Sally has hit the weekend she has already spent £168. This doesn't even take into account buying cosmetics, clothes or even spoiling herself with a facial.

Monday	£30.00
Tuesday	£26.50
Wednesday	£29.00
Thursday	£27.50
Friday	£55.00
TOTAL	**£168.00**

The scary thing is that Sally still has to pay rent, phone bills and her car bills. Oh and by the way, we haven't started on her Saturday and Sunday expenses. No wonder Sally finds herself desperately wondering week after week where all her money has gone.

The good news is that just a few small changes can make a big difference. Let's start with a tiny change — cutting out one coffee a day. Hardly worth the sacrifice? Does knowing that this one simple change saves £390 a year make you feel differently?

This exercise really opened my eyes. It wasn't until I broke down all my costs that I could see where all my money went. I can't believe that I could save so much just by cutting back on one coffee a day: £1.50 a day is not that much, but it adds up when you are spending small amounts all over the place.

I really wasn't thinking and I just got into the habit. I knew I was spending too much but I just couldn't see where. I am going to start by cutting back on one coffee and with the money I save I'll start to treat myself to a manicure once a week. **Sally, 31**

THEN THERE'S SAVVY GIRL SUSAN ...

Meanwhile, across town is a savvy girl by the name of Susan. Susan is saving for a holiday at the end of the year. She figures she will need around £750 for a week in Spain. This should be enough to cover her airfare and hotel and meals.

Savvy Susan earns the same salary as Sally; around £20,000. She works as an office administrator for an accountancy firm.

As you'll see from Susan's week, she is on target to save for her holiday.

MONDAY

8.00 am	Weekly travel expenses	£10.00
8.30 am	She grabs a coffee and heads into the office.	£1.50
9.00 am	To keep up with news, she buys the paper.	£0.50
11.00 am	Susan has recently discovered the benefits of herbal and 'chai' teas. She buys them from the supermarket and takes a supply to the office.	
1.00 pm	Each time she brings her lunch from home, she knows she is a step closer to Spain.	
6.00 pm	Having stocked up the fridge with plenty of groceries, she decides to make a chicken stir-fry, enough for two servings.	
	TOTAL	**£12.00**

It's the first day of the week and Savvy Susan is already ahead of Sally by £18.

TUESDAY

6.45 am	Half-hour run	
8.30 am	Susan is late this morning and has no time for breakfast at home. No drama, she has a box of her favourite cereal in the office. She grabs a coffee and heads into the office.	£1.50
11.00 am	Herbal tea time again	
1.00 pm	Lunch is last night's stir-fry and rice.	
7.00 pm	Susan needs a night out. Movie night; and she and her friends have a quick bite to eat beforehand.	£17.50
	TOTAL	**£19.00**

At the end of Tuesday, Savvy Susan is ahead by £25.50. What about Wednesday? Still on target.

WEDNESDAY		
6.45 am	Power walk (and good catch-up) with a friend	
8.30 am	She grabs a coffee.	£1.50
11. 00 am	Someone in the office is going out for coffees.	
	Today, Susan needs a lift and has a second coffee.	£1.50
1.00 pm	Susan brings a sandwich from home, but will buy a	
	freshly squeezed juice.	£2.00
7.00 pm	Gourmet Club Night:. it's Susan's turn to host and she is	
	supplying the cheese and bottle of wine. Everyone	
	will bring a platter.	£15.00
	TOTAL	**£20.00**

So far, she's ahead of Sally by £34.50.

As you can see, on average there's a saving of more than £12 each day between the girls. On Thursday Susan buys lunch and stays in the city after work for a drink with a friend who works nearby. On Fridays, like Sally, Susan wants to have fun and go out with her friends. Some of the best city bars offer 'happy hour' between 5 pm and 7 pm. The girls make the most of the cheap drinks, and then go out dancing or clubbing. Susan will likely spend around £30. Including her coffee during the day and sharing a taxi home, she'll have spent £35, a typical Friday for her.

Now, do you see where the money goes?

SALLY'S MONDAY TO FRIDAY		SAVVY SUSAN'S MONDAY TO FRIDAY	
Monday	£30.00	Monday	£12.00
Tuesday	£26.50	Tuesday	£19.00
Wednesday	£29.00	Wednesday	£20.00
Thursday	£27.50	Thursday	£15.00
Friday	£55.00	Friday	£35.00
TOTAL	**£168.00**	**TOTAL**	**£101.00**

Savvy Susan is 'saving' £67 a week. That's nearly £300 a month, or nearly £3,600 a year!

I really don't feel as though I'm missing out on anything. I just cut back on some of the little things and they all add up and they really make a difference. I don't feel like I compromise at all. Compromising for me would mean no coffee or juice, or not going out. Or worse still, living on peanut butter sandwiches every week! **Susan, 31**

If Sally could cut back on a few things, in four months she could take a trip overseas or buy that Whistle's dress she has been eyeing off. Or treat herself to a manicure each week or maybe a facial. The list is endless, and the savings are painless.

We've all had the experience of looking in our wallet and thinking, 'Where has all my money gone? I withdrew £50 only yesterday.'

13

This simple exercise will help you discover where your money is going. The time period over which you need to track your spending is one week, that's all. Just jot down what you spend day by day. Don't forget the £1.50 coffees or the other little bits and pieces. And don't think it's all just too hard.

Just think about all the time you've put in over the years counting calories and fat grams, keeping food diaries and doing complicated sums to find out whether you could have that chocolate brownie or not. This is so much quicker and easier than that. Spend just a few hours one night this week doing it and you'll find you will have already changed your life for the better!

HERE'S WHAT ANOTHER SAVVY GIRL HAS TO SAY

Brigitte is 24 years old and recently made a big move. She has set her sights on an overseas adventure.

I've recently moved cities and I share a flat with three other girls. The move has cost me quite a bit, but I have covered most of my expenses now.

I always take my lunch to work, that way I know what I'm eating. This can save me as much as £20 a week. I also walk home sometimes and that way I get my exercise in. It takes me 50 minutes from door to door. I don't walk in the morning, because I don't like getting sweaty.

I think I'm fairly good through the week. I like to save my money and go out on the weekends. A night out with my girlfriends costs around £25 to £35 for some food, drinks and taxis. It's great when I can share cabs with friends, but that doesn't always happen. Even so, I don't have a car so I figure I'm saving on that expense.

I buy really cheap shoes now. Once I spent £175 on a pair of boots and three weeks later the buckle broke and I paid an extra £25 to get it repaired. I'm happy with cheaper shoes and I'm really not into designer clothes at the moment. Don't get me wrong, I like them. I'm saving to go overseas, that is really more important to me than designer stuff.

Small things make a big impact

Brigitte's priority is an overseas trip and she has learnt how to cut back to make it happen. It's amazing how simple things, like cutting back on coffees, bringing lunch from home and walking instead of taking public transport can make the difference between being able to go overseas or not, or buying a decent car or not.

Look at just two simple changes.

Cutting back on one coffee a day @ £1.50 = £7.50 a week.

Multiply £7.50 by 52 weeks **Savings for the year: £390**

Cutting back on three bought lunches a week. (The other two days you can treat yourself.) 3 lunches @ £3.50 = £10.50.

Multiply £10.50 by 52 weeks **Savings for the year: £546**

Total coffee savings £390 + lunch savings £546 = £936

If you are becoming ever more conscious of how the little things add up, you're in good company. Madonna is famously careful not to fritter away her fortune on unnecessary purchases, and Catherine Zeta-Jones, one of Hollywood's best-paid actors and married to a multi-millionaire, says she is still 'thrifty by nature'.

If you are willing to cut back on three bought lunches and one coffee a day you can save over £900 a year. What else can you painlessly cut back on?

SOME OTHER EVERYDAY ITEMS

	Daily	Weekly
Magazines		
Chocolate bars		
Chewing gum		
Lotto and scratch cards		
Taxis (when you are too tired to		
wait for the bus or train)		
Dry cleaning		
Cigarettes		
	TOTAL	TOTAL

LET'S GO TO THE EXTREME

Life wouldn't be worth living if we cut out all the things we enjoy. But let's just take a look at what's possible.

We know Susan could save an additional £390 a year if she eliminated one coffee a day during the working week.

What about Sally? If she cut out both her coffees and brought her lunch from home, how much could she save in a year?

> Cutting back on two coffees a day will give her £780
>
> Cutting back on five lunches a week at an average of £4.50 each will give her £1,170
>
> **Total saving: £1,950**

Sure, this is an extreme case, and bringing your lunch every day may make you feel like you're back in preschool, but the point of the exercise is to show you how quickly little things add up. A couple of pounds here and a couple of pounds there — before you know it you've spent the equivalent of a complete wardrobe update, or a round-the-world air ticket.

If you really do value a coffee every day more highly than seeing Paris or New York, that's absolutely fine. But if you feel that no matter how hard you work you're barely staying ahead, then this is where to start. Cut out the little things you can do without and the big picture will look a lot brighter.

It helps to have a goal. When I was 20 I wanted to travel overseas with a friend. We decided we would save for a year and then have four months exploring India and

Thailand. When I started saving, I was tempted many times to buy a new bag, or go out for an extra night's clubbing. But when I felt myself weakening, I would say to myself, 'I can get the 1st class hotel (India style!) in Rajastan', or 'I'll be sunbaking out on a beach in Phuket.' I kept picturing myself in those wonderful cities I had dreamed of and the money went back in my purse.

My desire to see the exotic East and take four months off work was all the incentive I needed to get me there. And it was so worth it. Occasionally, my thoughts would wander back home as I lay back on my huge bed in an air-conditioned room or while I was sipping on a mai tai. I was so happy I'd stuck with my plan and saved. (By the way, did I mention the men in the nightclubs and sunsets on the beach?)

What are the things you want to look back on with pleasure five or 10 years from now? It all boils down to your priorities.

CHAPTER THREE

WHY DOES MONEY MATTER?

Well first there's that whole hopes-and-dreams thing! Being able to have the experiences you want, and own nice things is important for everyone. But being savvy about money is especially important for us women.

If being in debt doesn't worry you, your life must be a bit like Penelope's in our fairytale opening. Penelope is happy to max out her credit card because she knows her bills will be paid by her prince charming. The real world is different, and so are the lives of real women when the credit card bill arrives.

Take Linda's story below. After a failed marriage, she realised that it was up to her to take control of her finances. No longer did she have a partner to shoulder the debts.

Unfortunately I was only married for a short time, three years in fact. When my marriage ended I realised it was really important to stay on top of my bills.

When there are the two of you, you can rely on one another if you are short of cash or if a bill needs to be paid. It didn't take long before I realised that I just couldn't go out and spend on everything I wanted. I'm the only one responsible for my bills now. I began to wonder if it was going to be like this all my life.

I'll admit, I did go on a spending splurge when the marriage ended. I just needed to spoil myself. Then the bills came in. That was sobering. I really felt out of control, almost fearful, insecure and guilty.

Now after being separated for over a year, I'm making it on my own again, I have a good job, and I feel like things are back under my control. I feel confident, independent and secure. This is really important now because I'm on my own. **Linda, 35**

These days, we have to be smart about our money because we can't assume we're going to marry (let alone marry someone rich). In our lifetime, nearly 40% of British women will never marry. And of the marriages that do occur, sadly about half will end in divorce.

The reality will be that you may be on your own for a long time and even if you do marry or have children, you will still need to work. With this in mind, it is clear why becoming financially savvy is important for all of us.

It doesn't matter whether you've been in a relationship or on your own, debt can affect us all. After a career move Natalie went on a spending spree that took her into dangerous territory.

I found myself owing a huge debt, largely due to relocating for my new job. I was really excited about the move and I was looking forward to making a new start.

Unfortunately, I ended up buying a lot of new things and spending way over my budget. I was going out a lot, and because I work in the tourism industry I took up plenty of travel offers. The offers were really good value. I guess I just went overboard. Also, before I moved I had to buy a car because my job involved lots of driving. I applied for a £3,500 loan and bought a secondhand car.

After finding a new place to live, setting up the apartment with new furniture and adding this to my monthly car loan repayments and the credit card payments, I found my bills were getting out of control.

The debt I had gotten myself into started causing me lots of stress, and I couldn't believe how quickly it had mounted up. The worry I had over how I was ever going to pay the debt caused me to get really depressed and I couldn't sleep at night.

Luckily, a good friend suggested I go to my bank and see if they would extend the loan that I already had for the car. I was so grateful to the bank when they extended my loan and I was able to pay off the big bills, like my credit card and rent, which at the time were overdue by a few weeks.

I felt as if the whole world had lifted from my shoulders. Now I don't lose sleep at night, I realised I just went overboard. I don't want to be in that situation again. **Natalie, 33**

It's great to see Natalie has bounced back and is getting her eight hours' beauty sleep again. Like Linda, her sense of security returned once her finances were under control. Natalie's story is also a good reminder that if you do find yourself in a similar situation you too can turn things around.

There is no magic number – no pounds and pence figure – that implies you are in debt. That's because, as Natalie found, debt is when you are living beyond your means. It's not the amount you spend or what you spend it on; it's whether you can afford to pay it off. For example, you may have a debt of £1,500 or more on your credit card but if your salary comfortably allows you to pay this off at the end of the month, you're okay. If not, you are probably living beyond your means.

A much, much bigger debt – say £150,000 – can be okay if that debt is a mortgage and you are making your repayments each month. Why? Because you are investing in your future.

It all comes down to you taking a good look at your own financial situation. And to understand how you got there you need to look at the way you think about money.

MONEY BELIEFS

Have you ever thought about where your money beliefs come from? Were your parents conservative or careless with money? Perhaps they never spoke about it. Perhaps they made you budget your pocket money as a small child. Either way, rightly or wrongly, their beliefs may have influenced the way you handle your money.

For example, even though Julie doesn't regard herself as a money whiz, she has a father who made certain she developed the essential skills for practising good money management.

I wouldn't necessarily say that I am good with money, I just don't like being in debt. I've never had a student loan, bank loan or car loan, because I have never bought anything that I couldn't afford. I could happily live without a credit card. My dad always warned me about credit card interest rates and being in debt. He didn't believe in handouts, so I was never given any and I had to work for my pocket money when I was little.

It must be the way I was brought up as I have learnt to clear my credit card debt each month and I always pay my bills on time, so in that regard I never worry about money too much.

My partner is exactly the same, which makes our relationship easy. Neither of us is a big spender. We each pay our own bills and we pay the mortgage together. **Julie, 31**

Michelle has quite different habits. Now 26 and working for a fashion magazine, she has spending patterns that were entrenched from a young age.

Growing up, I always loved clothes. I would save all my pocket money and I would buy the latest clothes, lipsticks, anything that caught my eye. I had to have it. Today, things are not so different. I work for a fashion magazine and I am always surrounded by beautiful clothes, shoes and the models who make them look so great.

I have a wardrobe full of designer clothes. I love Jimmy Choo shoes, anything by Bella Freud, not that I can afford her clothes. But I would happily spend £350 on a pair of shoes I like.

I'll walk into a department store and spend silly amounts like £75 on a handbag or some lingerie. I say to myself, 'Just look.' But it is so tempting.

A couple of years ago I got myself into debt, so I took out a loan to pay off my credit cards. I had three credit cards and each one was carrying nearly £2,500 debt, almost £7,000 in total. I went to the bank and got a personal loan.

The interest rate on the personal loan was much lower than my credit card rate. It made a lot of sense to take out the loan and pay off my credit cards. I was surprised how good I felt, because I knew that I would pay off the debt within a year. There was no way I could have gotten on top of my credit card debts in a year if I hadn't taken out the loan.

Once I paid off the debt I kept two cards and cancelled one of them. I figured that two cards would help me to keep in control. When I had three I felt I had lots of money to play around with. It was just too tempting.

Now the two cards I have are getting up again. At least I know I could always go and get another loan. **Michelle, 26**

Michelle and Julie's stories show how much money affects your life and your chance to be happy. But they show something else too — how your past habits can predict your future ones, unless you are careful.

If you are feeling out of your depth and finding your spending habits are getting you down, you are not alone. Sandra has realised her financial status has a big effect on her happiness.

I can tell you that the number one feeling for me when I am in debt is depression and feeling limited, always having to budget. It's awful not having the freedom to get something that you see advertised or you need. You watch other people in shopping centres or on the streets with nice houses, clothes and cars and it's depressing.

You start to tell yourself that you could do better. But the reality is it's been the same for years and your hope diminishes because it seems so ongoing.

But when I pay my bills and pay my loan, I feel like I have made progress, even if it's only for a short time. It is such a great feeling to pay bills and be on top again. Just having money to buy something or even to go to the movies is a huge pressure release. **Sandra, 29**

While it's great that fashion addict Michelle took the initiative and paid off her credit card debt through a bank loan, her pattern of overspending is emerging again. And Sandra is making an effort too, but her old habits are still dogging her, making her lose heart.

You can't fool yourself by saying, 'It doesn't matter if I'm hopeless with money now. It'll all change. I'll wise up in my 30s, 40s or 50s.' It's a slippery slope to anxiety and unhappiness.

So how do you avoid that?

You might feel one day you are on top of the bills, then next day not. It's the money equivalent of yo-yo dieting: two steps forward, one step back. How many times have you tried to go on a diet and failed? I know, too many to count. But if you felt you absolutely *had* to lose weight to fit into a wedding dress, or a bikini for a special beach holiday, you would. It's all about your priorities and goals. Money works the same way.

Ask yourself, do I want to keep having the same issues throughout my life? And more importantly, can I ever change? The answer is yes, of course you can.

HOW TO BREAK YOUR BAD MONEY HABITS

Remove the temptation to shop

I understand it's hard if you work in the city or in a place surrounded by boutiques and department stores and you're wandering around every lunchtime being tempted. So what could you do instead?

- Read a book or a magazine in the park.
- Grab a coffee with a friend (this is still cheaper than shopping).
- Go for a walk – get your daily exercise in.
- Pay bills rather than create them. Do your internet or phone banking and get it out of the way.

The no-touch bank account

Set up a secondary bank account and have money automatically taken out of your pay and put into this account every payday. If you don't have the money in your hands, you're less likely to spend it.

Write down your goals, keep them nearby and check them regularly

The idea is to keep you focused on what you are saving for, whether it's a holiday, a party, a car or somewhere to live. Cut out a photo of what you're saving for and put it on a wall, near your desk or in your wallet. My next goal is a trip to Hawaii, so I have a photo of a tropical island as my screen saver.

Only take a small amount of money with you each day

Once you get into the habit of only taking a small amount of money with you, you'll find you spend less without even noticing.

Leave your credit cards at home

Again, remove the temptation. The world won't stop!

Power to the girlfriends

If you and your friends are in the same boat, then start working together and supporting each other. Check on each other's progress. You can do this even if you're just all trying to avoid accumulating more debt. But it's even better if you have a shared goal to work towards, for instance, a luxury weekend away in the country or even an overseas trip.

If your goals are the same you can track your savings together and encourage each other through the tough spots. When I went travelling with a girlfriend, we did just that, continually tracking each other's progress. We had a set amount that we had agreed we both had to reach before we could start our adventure.

Family support

Do you have a close family member or friend who is good with money? If you do then make a time to talk with them. Ask for some practical tips. If they know you well enough they may offer some tailor-made advice. Even just having them listen to your plans and act as a sounding board can be very useful. I do this with my family and friends, and I find it's really helpful to talk.

Just by making new spending habits today, you will change your future. Leave your old bad habits behind.

GOALS AND NECESSITY

My sister Rhonda was a classic spender. She loved clothes, nightlife, travelling, going out to movies and concerts. You name it, Rhonda spent her money on it. It wasn't until she decided to commit to her relationship that her priorities suddenly changed. These priorities have helped Rhonda form new habits that would take her into the future.

At the age of 31 her goals suddenly changed. She wanted to buy a new car, a two-bedroom flat and pay for a wedding. Within three years she has accomplished all three.

In 2002, my partner asked me to marry him. Well, that scared the heck out of me. After six years together I just thought, 'Why get married? We don't have any money, we have hefty credit card debts between us, we are still renting. How on earth are we going to afford a wedding?'

I had some coaching from Emily, and with her came up with a plan. 'Right,' I said, 'first things first. We have to get our financial act together to be able to afford a wedding.' We bought some simple money-tracking software and did a budget to see how much we needed to put away. Whoa! Even scarier than the thought of getting married was how much we needed to save! The wedding would have to wait for another 18 months.

We put the brakes on our spending, and started doing things like shopping on the weekend so we had food for dinners and lunches. We bought snacks to take to work from home, and eating out was cut down to once a week.

We used to like having breakfast out most mornings. Instead now we just have a coffee out together. The savings were really significant. Just the two of us cutting back on lunches saved £50 a week!

After getting used to the changes, including not having much money in our pockets, we started to see a dramatic increase in our savings. We were putting £50 away each week into a Lloyds savings account, and we did not touch it. The interest it earned helped too. We were still enjoying ourselves socially but within a few months we could see a big difference from those few small changes. Our savings were growing faster and faster.

We were saving so well I guess we got more confident about our ability to keep going, and we decided to look at property. So at the beginning of 2003 we approached half a dozen lenders and they all told us that we did not have enough saved for a deposit. But we were pleasantly surprised as to how little further we had to go and this was a huge motivation. By mid-year we had £15,000 saved and that was already more than 2/3 of what we needed.

For someone who took 34 years to get her act together I didn't do too badly! Now that I have all this, I think to myself 'I can afford to spend some money.' But then I say, 'What for?' This discipline is now instilled in me to keep that money growing for bigger things. **Rhonda, 34**

Rhonda's story is a classic example of how a person can change their past spending habits.

Remember no one is born savvy. I certainly wasn't. People change, and the two most common reasons for changing are chosen goals and necessity. Rhonda's reason was her goals. She could picture a new life and she wanted it badly enough to shake up all her old habits and make it happen.

For others it is a matter of necessity. That was the case with me — the necessity in my case was sudden retrenchment.

When I was 30 I was working for a leading advertising agency and my career was progressing wonderfully. I enjoyed my job and the challenges it presented. Rumours were rife that 11 people were about to lose their jobs but the account on which I worked was thriving, so I believed my job was safe. I can laugh now, but how naïve I was then. You won't be surprised to learn I was one of the 11, but I was completely shocked — I couldn't believe it. I found myself without a job, but with a mortgage and to make things even more interesting, discovered I was pregnant with my first child! Challenges? You bet.

In the end, I'm not sure whether it was through luck or perseverance, but I managed to find freelance work throughout the pregnancy, even if the work was sporadic. If it wasn't for the lessons I learned, my retrenchment would be a time in my life I'd rather forget. I felt weighed down with an overwhelming sense of financial uncertainty. What if my partner had lost his job? How would we have managed? The outcome was that I became determined to get my finances under control, and that's when my interest in investing began. I never wanted to be in that situation again. So for me the trigger to becoming financially savvy was necessity.

Sometimes life throws something unexpected your way and you may find you need to cut back due to a change in your lifestyle, like losing a job, getting ill or falling pregnant before you had planned. With some good advice and determination, you'll be able to see these hard times through.

Still, if I had to choose between goals and necessity to motivate me to become savvy, I would definitely choose goals!

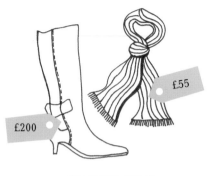

CHAPTER FOUR

CHARGING LIKE A WOUNDED BULL

Be honest, does your credit card bill make you feel a bit sick? Once you've taken a quick look at the amount due do you stuff the bill away somewhere and try to forget about it? It doesn't take long for bills to creep up, as Natalie found when she moved house.

Big expenses like moving house can do it, but so can updating your wardrobe too often, splurging at Christmas or even just letting everyday bills mount up. Before you know it you're over your limit and going backwards.

The term credit card has bothered me for some time. I think it's a total misnomer. How can it really be credit when the card is used to carry debt? Perhaps if we called it a 'debt card' people would understand what they are dealing with: a credit card is really just a collector of debts that need to be paid off monthly.

Maybe a 'financial health' alert similar to those about smoking and gambling should be imprinted on your card:

Warning: overuse of credit cards may cause bankruptcy

The problem with credit cards is that you don't see the exchange of cash. Imagine you have £200 in your wallet. With each purchase you see the money dwindling. Once there is no more cash, it's simple: there's no more spending. With a credit card the money is invisible. You hand over your credit card, you take your purchases and the friendly sales person returns your credit card intact. Nothing lost, plenty to gain as you happily walk out of the store with your bags of goodies. Until the dreaded bill arrives weeks later and suddenly your spending becomes a reality.

I don't know how many times I looked over my monthly credit card bill and only then remembered a particular purchase: oh yes, that petrol/book/dress — that's right, I put that on the card. Suddenly reality would sink in as my eyes scrolled down the list; once again I'd have spent more than I imagined. You've probably had similar experiences. Mary certainly has.

Mary loves clothes and she's paying a big price for indulging this love. High interest is keeping her from reducing her credit card debt.

I've got £2,000 debt on my credit card and I never manage to clear it. I think I pay around 14.9% interest on the card and I'll try to put a little bit on each month.

I love clothes, I'm a bit of a fashion victim. I buy my clothes from boutiques, eBay and from the markets. I recently bought a pair of shoes for £9 from eBay. It was a risk as I didn't know whether they would fit, but for £9 I took the risk and it paid off. I'll buy two or three pairs of new shoes a year as well and I'll spend between £100 and £150 for each.

I do mix expensive things with cheap things; you can do that with today's fashion. I don't earn much, but I do like clothes and that's where most of my money goes.

I share a one-bedroom flat with my boyfriend, and we pay around £250 a fortnight. We have been together for seven years and he is a better saver than I am. I just can't seem to save at the moment, though in the past I have saved for a trip to New Zealand. So I know I can do it if I really want to.

My boyfriend would like us to save for a deposit on a small flat. But I don't know if I want to give up the things I enjoy. It was different when I was saving for the holiday as it was only for a short time. If we buy a place I feel like I'll be saving and cutting back for 20 years or so. **Mary, 25**

SAVVY SOLUTIONS

Mary is carrying around £2,000 on her credit card from one month to the next and she's paying around 14.9% interest to do it. If she just maintains this debt without adding any new purchases she will be paying £298 a year in interest alone, without making any headway in paying off that existing debt.

There are a lot of things Mary could do with that £298 that would be far better than adding it to bank profits. It would cover the cost of two pairs of shoes each year, without compromising, or one fortnightly rental payment or a weekend away with her boyfriend.

It's great to see that Mary is not afraid to buy cheaper clothes if she really likes the look. But she does need to re-think her other financial choices. If Mary can't pay her credit card off then she will find it hard or impossible to ever buy a flat. It's very important to pay off your debts before you even consider investing.

So what can Mary do right now?

Just by filling out an application and changing to a lower interest rate credit card, she can instantly save hundreds of pounds a year.

By rolling her £2,000 debt over onto a credit card that charges 0% for nine months then 14.9% thereafter, Mary will pay nothing in interest payments, instead of the £298 she was paying on her old card. That's already a saving of £300, just by swapping cards.

HOW MUCH INTEREST DO YOU PAY ANNUALLY?

It can be quite a shock to discover you are paying hundreds of pounds each year in interest. Amanda did her sums and got a nasty surprise.

Due to a change in my finances and pay I was using my credit cards for just about everything, even for purchases as low as £5 or £7.50. I had two cards and over the course of six months my bills escalated and I had reached my cards' limit. I was finding it hard to pay my interest, which was more than £50 a month, let alone the whole bill.

I then realised that over a year I had paid roughly £600 in interest, I was horrified because when I thought about it I could have paid for a short holiday.

I decided to change to a lower interest rate credit card. So I swapped my credit cards, which had an interest rate of 16%, for the then newly launched Virgin card deal. It had an introductory offer of 0% p.a. for the first nine months, then 14.9% after that. I consolidated the two debts I had on my old credit cards onto the new one.

Swapping to the lower rate gave me the time I needed to get back on track without the added stress of that high interest rate each month. Credit cards are great, provided you trust yourself to make your payments a priority. **Amanda, 37**

If you don't know how much you are paying in interest, then get your most recent credit card statement and check it as soon as possible. Look down at the bottom line – the interest rate should be stated there. (If you are still not clear, phone your credit card company and have them clarify it for you.) It should also tell you on the statement how much you have paid in interest for that month. Multiply that figure by the number of months you've carried that debt over and you'll see the price you are paying for the card.

Virgin entered the credit card market in the UK five years ago, and they made things a whole lot better for everyone who has a card but doesn't pay it off in full each month. In keeping with Virgin boss Richard Branson's love of making a splash, the heavily advertised cards lured new customers with an extraordinary deal: no interest at all for the first nine months, then just 4.95% after that and no annual fees! (They also used marketing gimmicks like a choice of colours and a quirky shape.)

Not surprisingly the offer was a big hit. People switched over from their old high-interest cards as quickly as they could. Equally unsurprisingly, the smarter of the banks and other lenders were quick to follow Virgin's lead. Now there are quite a few options in low-interest cards. These institutions want your business so much they will offer you a 'honeymoon' rate so you can transfer your existing debt onto your new credit card and pay really low rates on that amount for a set period, often nine months, then pay a rate that is higher than this but still lower than your old card. Capital One takes a different road – no 'free' period, but a rate as low as 5.9% for the life of the balance transferred.

So if you are being charged anything above 13% interest and you're not clearing your whole debt every month, do something about it straight away. It's crazy to be making money for the banks when you don't have to.

As an example, if you have been paying 16% interest on a debt of £1,500, you can save around £180 just by transferring that balance to a new card with a 'honeymoon' interest rate of 0%. If you have more than one credit card you can consolidate them all and transfer the amount, saving you hundreds of pounds.

Currently, Virgin offers a 0% interest rate for the first nine months, then it jumps to 15.9%. This is still a good deal. (And by the way, I'm not on the Virgin payroll! I just have genuinely found their credit card to be way ahead of the banks.) But other credit card companies are aiming to match it, with MINT and Capital One particularly worth checking out.

SOME OTHER THINGS YOU CAN DO RIGHT NOW

Use the power of negotiation

With many customers now transferring their credit card debts to get better deals, the major credit card companies are now surprisingly willing to negotiate to keep customers. So even if you end up not switching, you can probably get a better deal, as Jenny did:

When I rang American Express to cancel my card, the lady I spoke to wanted to know why. I explained to her that I wanted to get a card with a lower interest rate and told her a friend had just applied for a credit card with a lower interest rate and recommended it to me.

I couldn't believe it when she then said that I had been a good customer and they were willing to forego my late payment penalty and my yearly membership fee if I stayed with them. Then she offered me two cinema tickets on top of that. I figured that this saved me a penalty of £40, and the annual fee of £40, plus throwing in two cinema tickets worth £25. The total came to £105.

I decided to stay with Amex because I thought she was doing her best to keep me as a customer and £105 was not a bad saving in fees for a year. **Jenny, 32**

This is not an isolated incident, so strike while the iron is hot. Let your card provider know you are shopping around and you might be pleasantly surprised by what they offer.

'CURRENT' NOT 'CREDIT'

You could learn to use a card that doesn't come with sky-high interest rates. It's your debit card.

Debit cards are issued when you get a bank account. They are used in exactly the same way as credit cards but only let you spend the money you have. They offer similar benefits to credit cards in that you don't have to carry wads of cash around. You can still pay your bills by phone or internet, and use them just about anywhere in the world, including to withdraw cash from ATMs in other countries. Of course, you will need to have sufficient funds or an overdraft allowance (a small one!) to cover your spending. That way you never have uncontrolled debt. The card accesses the money directly from your account. You will still receive a statement at the end of the month, listing all your purchases (it becomes part of your bank statement) and you can use it in a lot of situations, such as buying on the net.

Danielle found that her debit card works for her:

I don't have a credit card, what I do have is a multi-access debit card. So many times I have heard my girlfriends whinge about having £1,500 to £3,000 in debt on their credit cards and how they can never pay it off. What makes it worse is that their cards have been fluctuating like that for years.

For me, I believe if I don't have the money then I shouldn't be buying it. I also believe in out of sight, out of mind: if I don't have a credit card then I can't use one. I just don't get tempted. **Danielle, 25**

MANAGING YOUR CREDIT CARD

Credit cards are inherently useful. They allow us the freedom to make purchases when we are caught short. And should your wallet get stolen it's relatively easy to put a 'stop' on your credit cards, but just about impossible to recover a wallet full of cash. Also, for convenience when travelling overseas, credit (or debit) cards are essential. It's pretty much impossible to buy via the internet without a card. And, with more people working freelance or on short-term contracts, sometimes credit cards are very, very handy for bridging the gap between job payments. That's okay, as long as you are committed to paying off the cards once your next job comes through. Try explaining that to my father, though!

Dad asks a killer question ...

At the age of 77 my father was given an application by a shop he regularly visits for a store credit card. He was so baffled by the idea that it took us a long time to even explain the concept. He just couldn't understand that the card was used instead of money.

'Don't I pay for the clothes when I buy them?'

'No, Dad, you hand over the credit card and they will put it on a bill and send it you at the end of the month — then you can pay for it.'

'That's all I do, I don't hand over any money to the sales person?'

'No, Dad, that's why you have the card.'

'But I have to pay for it in a month? What's the use, I may as well pay when I'm there!'

Hard to argue with, when he put it like that ...

'Sure, my card debt is high, but I'm still saving'
You are probably thinking that you are doing the right thing by having some savings. That's certainly the case if you have no debt. But it is really important to pay off any credit card debt first, otherwise you pay more in interest than you make on those savings.

I do understand why it *seems* like a good plan to save: putting money away regularly on the one hand feels like it counters the debt you have on the other. You feel you're doing something right instead of just slugging away paying off debts only to end up back at zero. But in fact it doesn't make sense to have savings in the bank earning interest at 5% while you are carrying around £1,500 credit card debt at 16% interest.

Let's say you have £1,000 in an interest-bearing savings account that pays 5% annually. This will pay £50 interest and will give you a total of £1,050 after 12 months. But if your credit card is carrying £1,500 from month to month and you are paying 16% interest, the interest charged for the year will be £240.

The £240 interest you pay on your credit card is, in fact, eating into your savings. Your £1,050 is actually worth £810 because it's cost you £240 to make that extra £50. All your hard-earned interest and more has been lost because you have not paid off your credit card.

If you're in this situation, put this book down right now and transfer any savings towards paying off your credit card.

Check your fees as well as your interest rates

If you're even a day late with your credit card payment you could be liable for a penalty payment of £15 to £20. The same applies if you don't pay at all that month or, worse still, if you're even a few pence under your minimum required payment. So check what you're liable for, and at worst, make at least the minimum payment to cover you until you can sort things out.

Reward cards

There are a number of cards issued for the UK market where you can earn points or money-back offers when you use your credit card. Remember that you are spending money to earn less money so keep your spending habits in check! They are worth exploring, however, if you shop regularly at one kind of store or if you want to earn air miles to reduce the cost of your holiday flights.

www.find.co.uk lists some top rewards cards that come from as varied a range of sources as American Express, Marks and Spencers, British Airways, Conran, Homebase, Ryanair and others.

Typically, you earn points for each £1 you spend on your card to redeem when you make your next purchase. Others offer you air miles that will make your next flight that much cheaper (or even free if you have enough air miles).

Many others offer you 'cashback'. This works in a very simple way; for every £100 you spend, they give you back some money (often at the end of the year). For example, if the rate is 0.5% then for every £500 you spend, you get a £2.50 'reward'.

Golden Rule: These cashback offers are only of value if you pay off your credit card every month, so DON'T be tempted to try to earn cashback rewards if you are paying high interest rates and carrying over your debt — it isn't worth it!

WHICH CARD'S RIGHT FOR ME?

There are plenty of cards out in the marketplace and finding one to suit your spending habits is a step towards being money savvy. Money Supermarket is a website which provides free information (with easy-to-understand tables) on a number of financial services including credit cards. I've given a sample on the following page.

CREDIT CARD COMPANY	BALANCE TRANSFERS RATE AND PERIOD	NEW PURCHASES RATE AND PERIOD
VIRGIN	0% for 9 months	n/a
MINT	0% for 9 months	n/a
EGG	0% for introductory period (currently 9 months)	n/a
MORGAN STANLEY	0% for 6 months	0% for 6 months
MBNA	0% for 9 months	n/a
NATIONWIDE	0% for 6 months	n/a
HILTON	0% for 6 months	n/a
CAPITAL ONE	5.9% for the lifetime of the balance	0% for 6 months

TYPICAL ANNUAL RATE % (VARIABLE)	INTEREST FREE PERIOD (DAYS)	LOYALTY SCHEME
15.9	59	1 point for every £1 spent. Points can be spent in the Member's Shop
14.9	59	None
15.9	45	Up to 10% cash back from selected online retailers
15.9	55	None
15.9	59	None
14.9	56	Free extended warranty on gas and electrical goods costing over £50
15.9	56	2 points for every £1 spent. 3 points for every £1 spent at Hilton Hotels
12.9	54	Various rewards packages available

For other options check out www.moneymarket.co.uk, www.creditcardhome.co.uk, www.about-credit-cards.co.uk www.find.co.uk, www.fool.co.uk, or www.easy-quote.co.uk.

OUT OF SIGHT, OUT OF MIND, OUT OF TROUBLE

To get out of trouble, remove the temptation to spend.

Your credit card is like most other things in life: if you don't have it then you don't miss it. If you've decided that all you want to do is pay off your credit card bill then you can cut up the card, knowing that you can always apply for another one. Or, if that's too drastic, give the card to a trusted friend or family member until you have paid your debt.

And to make paying the debt easier, do what fashion addict Michelle did and apply for a personal loan to cover the full amount owing on all your cards, then pay off the lot.

SOME 'NEVER EVER EVER'S'

Never take up an unsolicited offer to extend your credit card limit, particularly if you are having difficulty paying off the full amount each month, no matter how much the bank encourages you with gracious comments. For example, 'As a long-standing loyal customer, we are offering you an increase on your limit.' Yeah, right. Tear the offer up immediately.

Never take out a new credit card and pay off the old one with it. Unless you can be guaranteed a very low interest rate for the first year to give you time to pay it off. And never ever play tag between existing credit cards, withdrawing money on one to pay another. If you do, you are moving into very dangerous territory.

Avoid withdrawing cash from your credit card. The interest is charged immediately (even if your card offers interest-free days on goods purchased) and can quickly hike up your interest payments each month.

TIPS TO KEEP TRACK OF CREDIT CARD DEBT

- Jot down the amount of your purchases in an organiser or your diary. Then at the end of each month add the figures up so you're not waiting until the bill arrives to find out what you need to pay. Or log onto the internet and check your statements online each week to keep track of your spending.
- Check your statements carefully. Make sure there are no surprises or overcharged amounts on your bill.
- Don't increase your limit no matter how enticing the letter of offer appears to be.
- To find out if your credit card matches the benefits of others available, you can visit the Money Supermarket website at www.moneymarket.com. The guide will help you find a credit card to suit your lifestyle.
- If you need to speak to someone who can objectively offer you some help, contact the National Debt Line on 0808 808 4000 or visit the Consumer Credit Counselling Service website at www.cccs.co.uk or Clear Start on 0800 138 5445.

£250

£150

CHAPTER FIVE

THE SEALED SECTION

There are some things that every savvy girl needs to know that really don't come up in polite conversation. Time for the hard facts.

MONEY, THE ROMANCE-WRECKER

Ah, falling in love. The swooning infatuation. You've met the man of your dreams and everything is going to plan ... until you discover your ideas about money and his are completely different. Unfortunately, money is right up there at the top of the list of reasons relationships break up.

You may remember, in Chapter Three Julie noted that she and her boyfriend have the same money beliefs, and this helps makes their relationship smooth. I'd go further than this, in fact a lot further. Money compatibility is crucial in a relationship.

Lucky Julie has found her match. But what if you're on the opposite end of the scale from your partner — he's a tightwad and you're the last of the big spenders? Or the other way around. If you don't deal with the differences early on, somewhere down the track you will have problems.

It is possible for such a relationship to work, but only if you're upfront about it and talk through your feelings, then reach an agreement about who pays for what, particularly if you are living together and paying bills together.

Sure, discussing finances with your partner can be tricky. It raises a whole host of sensitive issues, such as whether the person who earns more money has more say in financial matters. But ignoring it will lead to even trickier questions, like who gets the sofa when you split up?

One savvy suggestion is to have three different bank accounts: one account for each of you and a joint account. The joint account covers rent or mortgage, household expenses, groceries and other bills you split. You will need to agree on a percentage to take out of your pay packets each month to keep the joint account topped up. If you do it on a percentage basis then you are both contributing what you can, regardless of who earns more. You may, for instance, choose to deposit 60% of your pay packet; the remaining money you can use for your individual expenses, such as credit cards, entertainment or even investing.

Sexually transmitted debt

Everyone hopes that their relationship will last. But to protect yourself you have to remain financially savvy. The sad fact is that romance doesn't always work out. Just look around at some of the people in your own circle — girlfriends and family members — or think about your own past relationships. We need to be able to pick up the pieces if we find ourselves on our own.

What can you do?

Generally speaking, it's a good idea to know what's happening with your joint finances and to keep some financial independence within the relationship. You might feel at first that you are being disloyal by having your own savings account; you may worry that it looks as though you don't trust your partner. But that's the wrong way to look at it. You want the best for each other, right? Well this is the best way to ensure financial security for both of you. When you're celebrating your golden wedding anniversary you'll be glad you took care of the basics early on.

If you don't give yourself this level of security and something does, somehow, go wrong, you could end up with something that can be every bit as devastating as a sexually transmitted disease: sexually transmitted debt. This is when you are left with all his debts as well as yours after a break-up. You may discover unpaid bills that had been hidden from you or, in a worst-case scenario, your ex has suddenly disappeared, leaving you to try to pay massive debts you weren't aware existed.

No matter what your age or circumstances, anyone who doesn't take precautions can fall victim to a partner's debt, just like Melissa did.

Eight years ago I met the man of my dreams, or so I thought. I was 24 years old and he was 20. Around this time my career really took off. I was working in the hotel industry and I was required to travel a lot. I earned a good wage, in fact I was the primary earner when we decided to move in together. He was those few years younger, and I was a little concerned by this, but at the time he appeared mature for his age.

He had just started a full-time job, so I thought we could move in together and share the costs. Previously he was living with his family and I was renting on my own, so it made sense.

Whoever said love is blind got it right. Even though he was earning, he continually complained that he had no money. I thought his money was going into his car, but I later discovered when I was away travelling for work he was spending his money on going to clubs and taking drugs.

I had always been good with money and had very little on my credit cards. I paid all our bills. I even paid for his airfare so he could meet me on my work assignments abroad. How stupid was I? But he always said he would pay me back. And I was devoted to the relationship, so I thought it would work out in the end.

For our fourth anniversary, I paid the fares for us to take a short holiday. I ended up paying for everything. By now the habit had set in. At the time I also applied for another credit card. I loved him so much that I thought we would be together forever. The thought of us breaking up never entered my mind. I did think of the money he owed me from over the years but, as stupid as it sounds, I let it pass because I thought we would never part, that we would marry. Not long after that I discovered he was having an affair.

I bought him so much over the five years we were together. I gave him money all the time. Looking back now, after all the hurt and pain, I can see that it was partly my doing. I just kept applying for credit cards. They were so easy to obtain that after five years I had five credit cards plus loans covering the new furniture I bought when we moved in together. In total I had £10,000 debt.

My God, even as I tell this story again, I still can't believe how stupid I was. I'm a generous person and even when he was short of money and I knew he was hanging out with the wrong crowd and taking drugs, I didn't want to abandon him. I tried to help, even when he was sacked from two jobs. Even his own family told me not to give him any more money.

It was also hard to tell my family. Like I said earlier, I was always good with money and people used to ask me for loans. Now it was my turn. But once I told my family and friends, they were so supportive. They encouraged me along the way and helped keep me on track with my payments.

That was four years ago. Today I am much wiser and, in my mind, I know nothing is forever. The debt is almost paid off. I went to the bank and thankfully they gave me a loan of £12,000. I paid off all my cards and closed them all. The interest payments alone were killing me, I couldn't keep up.

I am almost there now. One more year and I will be free of debt and free of the bad memories of that relationship. Now I have a good job and I put £500 a month into clearing my debt – I have this automatically deducted. It has been a hard road but I am getting there, and the most important thing is that I'm happy and I can sleep at night.

Now I have no credit cards, just a loan that will be gone in one year. Then I can concentrate on buying a house. It's amazing how one person caused so much turmoil in my life, but I am also to blame.
Melissa, 33

I've known Melissa for a long time, and she's right when she says she was always good with money. If it happened to her it can happen to anyone — anyone who is trusting and too much in love to be suspicious.

It can certainly happen to older and wiser heads too. At the launch of *The Money Club* a woman approached me to tell me at the age of 65 she had finally found the courage to start investing. What led to her taking control of her finances was the death of her husband. During their time together he had always taken care of the bills — or so she thought. Only after he died did she discover they had a number of outstanding debts, amounting to thousands of pounds.

It came as a shock to her, but she had to deal with it. The first thing she did was approach her bank and explain the situation. Then she went about downsizing her house and car. With the money left over she paid off the debt, and for the first time started to think about investing. When I met her she had started an investment club and was feeling in control. This just goes to show that it's never too late.

A safeguard against sexually transmitted debt
Keep your credit cards in your name only and do not sign or guarantee another person's loan or credit card. If you do and that person is unable to pay their bills, the credit provider will come after you because, by acting as a guarantor, you have made yourself fully responsible to pay the entire debt.

The pre-nup
Pre-nuptial agreements are no longer just for the rich and famous. Anyone who has ever been through a separation and lost a lot of money in the process would agree with the benefits of having a pre-nuptial agreement.

If you think the divorce and family law courts will favour women after a break-up then you are kidding yourself. Men have long argued that they have been dealt a raw deal in the past and unfortunately this was probably true. But it's no longer the case. Recent changes in the divorce process mean that assets you brought into the relationship, children and their custody, pension plans, and each person's earning capacity, during and after the relationship, all go into determining who gets what.

In the UK, courts are not *obliged* to enforce pre-nups but they are now moving towards their acceptance and they will probably be taken into account if not enforced 'to the letter'.

The purpose of a pre-nuptial agreement is to protect the assets you bring into a relationship, particularly if you have more than your partner. Here's Carol's story:

I was married for nine years before we separated. My ex-husband and I had built up a very successful business and when we split, I was determined to look after the assets I had gained during our marriage.

I wasn't looking for another relationship, particularly after a messy divorce. Unfortunately, when there is a lot of money at stake, it tends to be that way. I wanted to try to get back to a normal life with our three children.

I met my second husband quite by accident. He worked at my local bank and we started seeing each other. After a year we decided to move in together. I had a lot more assets than he did and we decided he would move into my house as it was much larger than his apartment.

Perhaps it was because he was in the finance industry that he was very understanding when I talked to him about our finances. Mainly because I had a lot more to lose than he did, I wanted to make sure my assets and my children were protected should we go our separate ways.

We put everything in writing. Basically if we break up we keep everything that we brought to the relationship. The things we accumulate together we would split according to who wanted it more, or who paid for it. He was really great about the whole thing. I guess that's another reason why we ended up getting married. **Carol, 36**

UK GOVERNMENT LEGAL ADVICE SITES
www.direct.gov
www.adviceguide.org.uk
A GOOD COMMERCIAL SITE
www.legal-advice.co.uk
A USEFUL SITE
www.clickdocks.co.uk

COVER YOUR GREATEST ASSET

Invincible, that's what you are, right? You have the freedom to come and go. Your career funds the lifestyle you have become accustomed to. Friends and family are always behind you. Life is looking pretty rosy, until ...

It's breast cancer awareness month and you decide to heed the message and do the right thing, so you visit your doctor for a breast examination.

Your doctor begins the examination, and stops suddenly. Your heart stops too, then accelerates as she recommends you have a mammogram as soon as possible. The unthinkable happens and a lump is detected; in an instant, life has changed. You need time off work. Surgery, chemotherapy and recovery are now the priority in your life.

We know it is a tough battle fighting a disease like cancer, but if you are struggling to make ends meet the impact is so much worse. How are you going to cope?

The events above really happened to two good friends of mine. Luckily they both had an income protection insurance plan that helped them through.

If you imagine it won't happen to you, stop and think for a minute. Both my friends were at the peak of their careers and were fit and seemingly healthy. Just look around at your friends and colleagues. You probably know someone who has had a life-threatening illness or other major health scare. Even the rich and talented are at risk:

Anastacia and Kylie Minogue are two women who have found themselves battling life-threatening diseases, both taking time out of their careers to recover.

Any number of illnesses or injuries can stop you in your tracks. Statistics suggest that up to half of working Britons will have a minimum of three months off work at some point due to an illness. Women in particular need to come to terms with this reality, especially when they are helping to support children or are the sole breadwinner.

Imagine being struck down by a serious illness when you're on your own with a mortgage. It happened to Penny:

I was going through a difficult time, and I had been under a fair amount of stress at work. There were a lot of deadlines to meet and the pressure had been building up. I started to notice that I was getting sick often and had to have a few days off work.

One day I was walking along the street and my legs gave way on me. This was the beginning of a nightmare that has been with me for the last two years. I could not get up and sat on the pavement for some time. I then phoned a friend, who came immediately and took me straight to the doctor.

I notified my employer and they were really understanding and supportive, but what followed were months and months of medical tests. At one stage I was wheelchair-bound and I thought I was never going to walk again. I was so worried about my job and how I was going to survive. I had a mortgage, but luckily I had taken out income-protection insurance when I started my job. I work in the finance industry and I guess I'm more aware of what cover is available than most people. I have both income-protection insurance and life insurance.

The insurance means that if I become temporarily or permanent disabled, I'll get some benefit from my insurer.

Not for one minute did I think I would ever really need this insurance, certainly not so soon. I'm only 33 years old. I just got it because now that I have a mortgage I do tend to worry a little more, plus I'm on my own. I'm conscious that I don't have anyone to fall back on.

The killer with my insurance policy was I had a 90-day waiting period before I got any money. But luckily I'd some savings put aside so I could survive on this money before the policy finally kicked in and my payment came through. It has been a lifesaver. I don't know what I would have done or how I would have survived without it. Almost a year after my initial collapse they discovered I have a muscular disease, which continues to plague me.

I have returned to work now. I started with three short days a week and now I'm almost back to full-time. I can't do the things I used to do, like run or walk too far, and I do have relapses. Sometimes I can't get up out of bed because of the muscle pain. I'm limited, but at least I was able to have time to recover, keep my job and pay my bills, thanks to my income-protection insurance. **Penny, 33**

What to look for in income-protection insurance

Income-protection policies are generally offered by life and health insurance companies.

Make sure you are being covered for the work you perform. Define your income-producing duties. Ask yourself are there any illnesses that you are not covered for? Make sure you receive this information in writing and find out how long the waiting period is: for example, 90 days before you receive a payment.

Most policies should be able to provide you with an ongoing income: up to 75% of your salary.

As your salary increases, check that your payments and projected payouts also increase.

If you aren't working full-time, you should check that your company will cover you – some policies don't cover part-time workers.

For more info visit www.lifeassure.co.uk. This site can help you estimate the cost of your premium. And you should bear in mind that income-protection insurance is tax deductible.

If you have a complaint about insurance, contact the Financial Services Authority (FSA) on 020 7066 1000 or go to www.fsa.gov.uk

DO YOU HAVE MILLIONAIRE CHARACTERISTICS?

Ever wanted to know what makes a millionaire and how they succeeded? American author Thomas Stanley interviewed more than 300 women who became self-made millionaires. In his book *Millionaire Women Next Door*, Stanley studied ordinary women who became wealthy.

He identified some characteristics that they all had in common.

Check to see if you share them.

I. Perseverance. Whatever idea the women had, they persevered, no matter what anyone said and regardless of what happened. For anyone who is in the process of starting their own business, perseverance is the number one characteristic needed. Look at your favourite Olympic athlete if you need an inspiration boost: would they be where they are today if they gave up after each bad training session or race they lost? You can accept no boundaries if you wish to succeed. You must believe you can do it.

2. They receive tremendous satisfaction out of owning a business, achieving, learning and making other people happy. And in many cases this substitutes for high consumption and spending. The feeling of achievement you get when all your hard years of study pay off on graduation day, or when you land a great job, or win someone's business you've put yourself on the line for, is one you simply can't match by accumulating possessions or partying. You can't put a price on that feeling.

3. They were not all gifted and they were not always even the smartest person among their group of friends. Bill Gates, the Microsoft founder, didn't even graduate from college. Instead he devoted his time to computer work, something that he was passionate about. This passion and perseverance has

made Bill Gates one of the wealthiest men in the world.

4. Even after they made millions, they were still frugal with money and continued to live within their means. Some still use discount coupons and shop at bulk discount stores. This is understandable if you started with nothing and then made a lot of money. If you've done it the hard way, it's easy to remember what it was like to struggle financially. And a true bargain is still a bargain no matter how much money you have.

5. More than 20% of the millionaire women interviewed were originally teachers. This makes sense as teachers usually need to be well disciplined and intelligent. Also, they take the initiative and are usually very frugal — they have to be, since their work is underpaid and their schools are often under-resourced. I take my hat off to teachers.

6. They were in the right profession to make the most of opportunities. Professions that lend themselves to young women becoming moguls are real estate; recruitment; business management; and childcare proprietor.

YOUR BIGGEST HIDDEN ASSET

You could probably write a page-long list of your assets without hitting on one that is vital, but often forgotten: your pension. If you have done nothing in regard to investing or even putting money aside for a rainy day, then your pension will be all you have to fall back on.

It's hard to imagine or even take an interest in your pension when you are in your 20s, but things really change when you hit your late 30s and 40s. You begin to wonder, 'Will I have enough to retire on?', 'Have I contributed enough?' Jobs may become more precarious as you get older.

'The only time I think about my pension is at tax time'
One of the benefits of making regular pension payments is that they are pre-tax, saving you up to 40% more than if you saved out of your post-tax income (i.e. what goes into your bank each month) and you don't even notice it coming out of your salary. Like Debbie, you may only think about it once a year:

It's a bit embarrassing because I only think about my pension at tax time. I don't even know what kind of account I have. I actually forgot who my pension fund was last year.

I don't know anything about pension funds, even though I've got some. I know employers help you choose between different pension funds for you and you get these statements. A year ago I was talking to our accountant from the office and he was discussing pensions. I asked him, 'What's a good type of pension fund?' I've got one pension account with Standard Life that was set up when I was with my first employer and I have been contributing to this with my current employer.

The accountant said because I am young I should opt for a high-risk fund. The returns may fluctuate from year to year but he said I won't notice it, and if I lose a bit one year, I'll make it up another year. This makes sense because I don't see or miss the money, so I can take risks over the course of my contributing years. This could be as much as 40 more years. I'm *definitely* going to pay more attention to it in future. **Debbie, 25**

Why you should think about additional contributions

Women in particular are more likely to be out of the workforce for periods at a time, having children. When women return to work our earnings are often reduced because we choose to work part-time or end up working on contract, with no pension. We often miss out this way in comparison to men.

While you are young and earning solidly it's worth considering putting a little extra away, particularly if you may take time out of the workforce later.

There is currently no obligation in the UK to put money away into your own pension fund. However, pensions are a real stress point at the moment for everybody and the UK Government is considering a compulsory pension contribution scheme similar to the one enforced in Australia; there, a certain percentage of your salary automatically is taken from your pay or wage each month.

However, it is worth saving now, even if you don't have to! There are tax benefits to be had anyway.

If your company allows and encourages pension payments from your salary, you should almost certainly say 'Yes, please'. Money will be taken from your salary before you pay tax so you are effectively saving 25% more than it is directly costing you if you are taxed 25%, more if you are a higher-rate tax payer. The great thing is that you don't really miss it when the money is taken out before tax, it all adds to building your nest egg.

Then there are things called Additional Voluntary Contributions or 'AVCs'. The same tax benefits can apply so you ought to look at what you could salt away now (even if it's only £10 per month). It all adds up and you might be really glad later!

Think about it. If you can actually have £1.25 for every £1 you put into your pension fund, even if you can't get to it until you retire, that is a great deal.

How much do I need to retire on?
Retirement seems such a long way away. But think about it for a minute: how much would you need to live on? Of course the ideal amount depends on many things, but mostly it's about the lifestyle you want.

The figures below give you an indication of the size of the lump sum you will need to have when you retire to generate the annual income you want. (It's calculated on a lump sum pension payout on retirement and earnings of around 6% to 7% a year.)

£165,000 will generate £10,000 a year

£240,000 will generate £15,000 a year

£410,000 will generate £25,000 a year

£500,000 will generate £30,000 a year

If you're looking at these figures and saying 'There's no way I could live off £10,000 or even £20,000', all of a sudden retirement money issues start to become more real, even though it won't happen for decades. This is the best time in your life to do something about it — when you're 50 you'll never be able to catch up. Start by adding more voluntarily into your pension fund, Additional Voluntary Contributions or 'AVCs' or at least keep up your pension contributions even if you are in and out of the workforce.

Bear in mind, when they retire most people will own their home and car. Their kids should be off their hands. But the bills still come in, and you do not want to be trying to live on just a government pension, trust me.

Making some sense of the options on pensions

If you are lucky enough to work for a company that has what is called a 'Final Salary Scheme' you really must look at this and make maximum use of their offer. In these schemes your pension will be a percentage of the last salary you receive before you retire (usually about 50%) and they are almost always the best option by far. Because they are such good offers, however, most such schemes are now closed to new entrants and if you aren't already a member you won't be able to join.

The next 'layer' of the pension cake is the so-called 'Stakeholder Pension'. Here you set up your own pension 'savings' account (with tax benefits that you can take advantage of) with one of the big pension companies such as Standard Life or Prudential. You will contribute a pre-agreed amount each month (or week if you prefer) until you retire, and then get a monthly 'annuity' from that moment until you die. If you save more now, the annuity will be bigger, of course. You will also have the option of taking out a lump sum at retirement in exchange for a smaller monthly annuity; you may choose to do this to pay off any remaining mortgage owed, for instance. How much you get will also depend on how much your fund has grown and on interest rates at the time of your retirement. You can change what your fund is invested in at any time and you should keep an eye on this at regular intervals. You need to do some research before you sign up to make sure the fund you choose has a good track record.

I really want to emphasise that if at all possible you shouldn't rely on the basic state pension that you will be entitled to from your 'normal' tax payments made during your working life. At around £160 per week it isn't very generous and won't cover very much — just read the papers and look to see how many stories there are about pensioners on the state pension who can't pay heating bills or house repairs or all the other things that are difficult enough for us all even when we are earning a regular wage!

There are some excellent websites for some initial research and then you should see an Independent Financial Advisor (see Chapter 9) to get a lowdown on the best pension plan for you.

Websites that you might like to look at are:

www.pensionguide.gov.uk

www.opas.org.uk

www.stakeholder-pensions.org.uk

www.adviceonline.co.uk

CHAPTER SIX

YOUR MONEY HOROSCOPE

Ever wondered what the stars say about you and your money habits? Astrologer Kelly Surtees takes a close look at what your star sign reveals about your money personality. Are you indecisive or diligent when it comes to handling your finances? What traps do you have to watch out for? And what are the financial strengths you may not even know you have?

ARIES: 'CONFIDENT AND CRAVES INSTANT GRATIFICATION'

21 March–20 April

By nature this Mars-ruled sign is impulsive, courageous, impassioned and inspired. Aries individuals tend to act first then think later. They are confident about taking the initiative.

The 'I-want-it-now' drive of Aries translates to a desire for instant gratification, and with credit card at the ready it's all too easy. First step for you, Aries, might be to leave the credit card at home (remember, out of sight, out of mind).

The courage Aries is known for gives you strength and confidence to make changes and take charge regarding investments. While other signs may endlessly deliberate about the merits, or lack thereof, of certain investment opportunities, you possess an innate understanding that the only true way to find out what works or doesn't work is to give it a try. Your inspiration and dreams for something more than what you have today mean you are happy to wear a loss. You would rather have given something a shot than done nothing at all.

Your short attention span and responsive nature may, however, see you chopping and changing between investment products or stocks more often than is wise. Embracing the lesson of patience regarding investments will be your most valuable investment decision.

TAURUS: 'HAPPIEST SURROUNDED BY BEAUTIFUL THINGS'

21 April–20 May

Ruled by Venus, you are easily enticed into spending money on beautiful things, body treatments, clothes and decorations for the home. Anything that helps to make you or your space prettier is an easy sell when you are around.

Taurus is known as one of the money signs, for as much as you spend, you are also quite good at making money. (Phew!) The pleasurable things in life are worth spending money on, according to you. Generally, big expenditures are easily handled by your steady Earth energy. As a fixed sign you find it easy to commit long term to financial plans. Finding the freedom within your big plans for a little retail therapy here and there helps you maintain control.

The Taurus energy is associated with the farming cycle – building each year on what you have achieved in the previous one. This mentality is great when applied to your savings plan. You understand that saving even a little today makes for a lot tomorrow. Money seems to flow around you – plenty coming in and going out. The trick for you is to siphon a consistent amount into long-term financial investments.

With your slow and steady nature, the time required to make a financial plan bear fruit is usually not a barrier. Coming to grips with the reality that a mortgage or savings plan doesn't mean no shopping (just less) is a big step towards financial independence for you!

GEMINI: 'INDECISIVE AND A WORRIER'

21 May–21 June

Easily influenced and quick to change, Geminis have a hard time settling on the idea of setting up a financial plan, let alone deciding what investment avenues to follow. Your tendency to worry and feed yourself excessive amounts of information is best put to rest by employing a trusted financial advisor or planner.

A view of the bigger picture of your overall plan will keep you focused on moving forward instead of getting caught up in today's current favourite investment option. Unless you are specifically educated in the field of money management you will do well to have a professional provide information for key decisions.

Your constant umming and aahing about which choice to make could mean you sometimes miss opportunities. Your natural curiosity can run amok and see your investments spread too thinly across a wide range of options. Obtaining some professional advice will help you narrow down your investment scope while still maintaining some diversity. Your natural desire for different interests shows you are comfortable with the concept of diversifying and picking appropriate investment options for your personal situation.

CANCER: 'SWAYED BY EMOTIONS AND A SMALL RISK-TAKER'

22 June–22 July

As a sign concerned with protection, you will naturally be looking for safer or lower risk investments to protect your underlying capital. High risk or speculative choices will have you feeling out of your depth. Finding investment choices that have a lower risk will leave you feeling safe and in control.

In money management, as in life, rewards can sometimes only be gained by taking at least a small amount of risk. Your confidence and ability to extend yourself in the financial world is linked to your confidence and your ability to take risks. You are a sign easily swayed by emotions. Particularly when it comes to the all-important home purchase, you will need to take care that your emotions don't interfere with your budget. Having a trusted friend or advisor to help keep you focused on the financial aspect of a decision is important.

Ruled by the Moon, your feelings ebb and flow like the tides, and separating emotions from money-related decisions will be a key factor on your journey to financial independence. Family may have a big influence on your money beliefs. Just remember, even though they are family members their situations will differ from yours.

LEO: 'A SHOW-OFF WHO LOVES MATERIAL OBJECTS'

23 July–23 August

As one proud individual you like to surround yourself with material objects that you can show off. This can lead to a tendency to overspend on some of the more discretionary items like clothing, your home, car and jewellery. With self-esteem so linked to what others think of your appearance, your budget can blow out at the mere mention of an important function or social event.

Disconnecting from what others think about how you dress, the car you drive or where you live will be a key step in you curbing some of your excessive spending. While financial investments are nowhere near as glam as a prestige car or designer handbag, they will set you up for a stronger platform to treat yourself in the years to come.

Like your fellow fixed signs Taurus, Scorpio and Aquarius, you tend to over-think or plan. Sometimes this leads to you missing key investments because you feel like you need even more information. Allow the fiery energy running through your veins to take charge and make a decision. Your natural leadership skills mean you won't feel like you have to wait until all your friends get into the housing market or investment field before you do — instead of trying to set trends in the glamour stakes, why not lead the way into the investment world?

VIRGO: 'EXCESSIVELY ANALYTICAL, AND MAY MISS THE BIG PICTURE'

24 August–22 September

Meticulous and famously detail-orientated, you are extraordinarily well ordered. Your ability to set up systems and run processes is second to none in the zodiac, and when applied to your bank balance will be a great gift. However, one trap that many Virgos fall into is the 'failure-to-see-the-wood-for-the-trees syndrome', where the small details become such a focus that you forget to keep sight of the bigger picture.

Keeping an eye on an ultimate long-term goal will help prevent you from excessively analysing the little steps that you are taking to get there. Sometimes life will distract you from where you are going, and small adaptations need to be made in the realm of the everyday. But if you are able to keep moving towards a final goal, the worry that plagues you so often will dissipate a little.

You understand that information-gathering and research are necessary, but don't need to be taken to extremes. Your willingness to apply your keen planning and organisational skills to your money management is a measure of how successful you will be on the road to financial independence.

LIBRA: 'INDECISIVE AND GENTLE BY NATURE'
23 September–23 October

The biggest financial challenge facing you is the indecisiveness that is known to plague those born under your sign. The need to weigh up options from all angles sometimes means you miss the action (because come deadline day you're still debating the pros and cons).

Your gentle nature means that you sometimes lack the assertiveness to push yourself ahead of the pack in the financial world. Your strong desire for fairness is of no use when it comes to money management, as not everyone is a winner in this game. Allowing yourself to succeed where others may not will be a big step forward for you. It is okay to achieve on your own — don't be held back waiting for everyone else to get their act together.

What may work very effectively for you, Libra, is to get together with an investment group or organisation that will allow you to surround yourself with like-minded people and encourage you to make decisions and move forward towards your goal of financial freedom.

SCORPIO: 'STUBBORN, BUT MONEY SAVVY'

24 October–22 November

You are commonly referred to as the Sun sign with the most canny money-managing skills. Your ability to work effectively with the resources you have at any point means you are constantly looking ahead financially. Money is one subject with which you are comfortable.

You are quick to recognise there is a certain amount of power and freedom that comes from having a solid financial base. What may hold you back is your stubborn, fixed nature that wants to explore all possibilities before acting.

Your tenaciousness when it comes to thoroughly researching investments will serve you well on the large and slower paced investment styles. Your ability to take a long-term view means that you are happy to miss out on small gains today in the hope of larger gains down the track. You may be rather suspicious of any short-term, flavour-of-the-month investment vehicles that come your way, which is not necessarily a bad thing.

Your nature is more comfortable with big-scale, future-orientated investments.

SAGITTARIUS: A 'DON'T-FENCE-ME-IN' ATTITUDE REQUIRES A SAVINGS PLAN
23 November–21 December

Happy-go-lucky and freedom-loving, you are more concerned most of the time about where and when the next adventure will start. Money only comes into the equation as a means to an end. Motivating yourself through travel or study goals will help you stick to a more mundane savings plan.

Ruled by Jupiter, planet of optimism, you have little desire to plan much for the future on any level, preferring to trust that you will always land on your feet. And in many areas of life you will. However, a solid financial platform doesn't fall from the sky (unless of course you have some ageing relatives ready to leave their fortune to you!). Getting your head around the fact that putting something away today means more travel or freedom in the future will get you started. Realising that a mortgage is a step towards that extended overseas trip (you can always rent the property out), and not a ball and chain weighing you down is a good beginning. Look for investments that won't curb your spontaneous lifestyle too much today, but allow you to put money away for an even more freedom-filled tomorrow.

CAPRICORN: 'PRACTICAL AND DILIGENT, YOU TAKE THE LONGER TERM VIEW WITH SAVINGS'

22 December–20 January

Known for your steady and practical nature, you always have your eye on your current financial status. You take a longer term view than most and have an innate awareness that money doesn't grow on trees. Instead it must come from a little diligence and saving.

With your cautious, and at times reserved, nature you will be looking for more traditional styles of investment. Perhaps investment options that worked for your parents, those tried and true money-makers, like property, are where you are likely to be comfortable putting your money. The new investment products may confuse you a little, but if you apply your dogged research capabilities to reading the fine print you may find these modern investment products have something to offer. If you choose to apply your management and organisational abilities to your finances you will be well on the way to financial freedom.

A financial plan is similar to a business plan and if you add it to your list of 'To Do's, you'll find yourself making a priority of managing your money.

AQUARIUS: 'AHEAD OF THE REST WHEN IT COMES TO MONEY'

21 January–17 February

You are known for your ahead-of-the-times ideas and you may struggle to understand where the rest of us are at, in terms of money management. Your concepts usually go way ahead of what is on offer today, as the mass only moves at the speed of the slowest mind.

What you will need to do in order to build financial security for yourself is stop trying to force everyone else to move at your pace and instead look for innovative ways to work around what is currently available in the investment world. Your high level of intelligence would rather be put to use on humanitarian projects or cutting-edge technology, as the mundane everyday demands of life lack the spark to keep you interested for long. However, once you set your mind on something you are likely to see it through.

Find ways of making investing inventive and you will find your interest and commitment levels rise. You will benefit greatly from a trusted advisor who will integrate some of your more left-field ideas into today's investment options.

PISCES: 'DREAMY, YOU STRUGGLE WITH POSSESSIONS AND MATERIAL THINGS'

18 February–20 March

Your dreamy nature is not the best for meeting the demands of money management. However, one thing that is often overlooked when traditionalists describe your sign is the innate ability Pisceans have for working with power.

In our modern society, money very much equals power and you have an inner ability to attract just what is necessary to you at the right time financially. Like your fellow Jupiter-ruled Sagittarians, you tend not to plan for the future, trusting it will take care of itself.

Pisces really struggles with possessions and so you lack the desire for buying things that motivates so many people towards financial freedom.

What your Piscean mind needs to grasp is that money, and a solid financial base, also equal freedom – something you long for deeply. With some money behind you, you would be able to travel on a whim or take a sabbatical from work to pursue more spiritual or esoteric pursuits. You may need to employ an earthy advisor to keep you saving regularly, but keeping the ultimate goal of personal freedom in your mind will keep you moving on the path to financial independence.

Kelly Surtees is a professional astrologer who combines traditional and experiential techniques to bring astrology alive for each individual. For more information visit www.kellysurtees.com.

CHAPTER SEVEN

THE GIRLS MAKE HEADWAY

In Chapter Two we discussed cutting back on some of the smaller expenses to save you thousands of pounds over the course of a year. Did you manage to find areas where you could cut back? If you have but you're still looking to save a bit extra then here are some more ideas you can put into place right now.

As you've seen, the scale you're trying to save on doesn't matter — whether it's just trying to make ends meet or saving for the latest Jimmy Choo shoes, a holiday, a car or even a property, you can begin to make these small changes without too much compromise. These stories show how easy it is and how great it will make you feel.

DAY-TO-DAY TIPS

I'm not a heavy smoker by any means, but I do like to smoke when I go out with my girlfriends. I figured by cutting back on a packet of cigarettes a week, I was already saving £5, or close to £30 a month. I decided I wanted to give it away because I was scared I would want to have more and become addicted and then it would cost me hundreds of pounds a year. I'm glad I quit before it got to that stage – not to mention the health side of things. **Louise, 24**

I try to buy clothing that doesn't need to be dry-cleaned. Not only am I saving the cost of dry-cleaning, I also don't have the hassle of remembering to drop them off and pick them up. **Josephine, 35**

When my partner and I decided it was time to stop paying rent and buy a place of our own, the first thing we did was download one of those budget planners you find on the web. We chose one that was on www.bigall.com. It was a great help because we needed to find out where our money was going before we could find ways to cut back. **Lucy, 26**

I really believe that starting small is a good way to start saving. When I went through my bills, especially my phone bill, I saw that I was paying £1.75 a month to have 'call waiting'. I decided to ditch this cost, because I figured if someone really needed to talk to me they would call back. It's a tiny amount, but still, there's £21 a year saved without me even noticing. The other thing I did was to cut back on newspapers and magazines. I know it's not much, but I would spend around £20 a month on newspapers. What I do now is just get the Sunday paper and I'll read the daily papers in our office. **Angela, 27**

I have had to move apartments a number of times and I find that each time I move I end up with a lot of stuff that I've bought or just accumulated. What I have done twice now is have a garage sale. The last one I had was with a girlfriend who had just broken up with her boyfriend and she wanted to get rid of a lot of stuff and move into a smaller place. With two of us, we shared the advertising cost in the local paper and we pocketed around £100 each for the day's work. It's such a relief to get rid of stuff and not have to cart it into the new place. **Dianne, 35**

One thing I make sure of is having enough food in the house for the week. I will shop on the weekend and buy things like snack bars and enough bread to make sandwiches. I also buy things like Lean Cuisine meals for those nights when I don't feel like cooking. It's still cheaper than eating out or getting takeaways. It just takes a little planning at first. Now I'm used to it, it's just second nature to make my lunch. I know I have saved hundreds of pounds over the last two years. I'm saving because I want to buy a flat. **Alana, 33**

I have money automatically taken out of my salary and put into a savings account. I never see it, so I don't miss it. **Louise, 26**

Many years ago I heard someone suggest putting money aside in designated envelopes would help to pay bills. Basically, once you got paid you straight away put the money aside in a separate envelope for each bill that has to be paid for the month, before you have time to spend it. I thought this was a good idea but a bit too structured for me. What I do is have two jars and at the end of the week I take the loose change from my wallet and put this into the jars. One jar I have labelled 'shoes', the other is for going-out expenses. I'll put more away in the going-out expenses jar, only because I dip into it more than the shoe jar. I always need a new pair of great shoes each season and the money I save in the jar just about covers the cost. **Alice, 33**

I really like the idea of taking the loose change from your wallet each week. It may seem minuscule but over time it adds up. Many years ago I met a guy who'd done just that. Each week he put his loose change in a bottom drawer. When he discovered he was about to become a father he decided to put the money into a savings account for his child's education. Without fail, each month for 20 years, he would put his monthly haul of change into the account. The money he saved plus the interest he earned on it was enough for him to pay for his son's education.

I used to spend a lot of money on clothes but then I stopped. Mainly because my best friend moved overseas, and shopping wasn't as much fun without her. I'm just not a brand person and could never spend £100 on a pair of shoes, but we used to visit op shops and markets together and we both loved bargains. It's just not fun in the same way when she's not around. I've never saved so much, and now I'm planning to go overseas next year to meet up with her. **Tara, 26**

While it's a little drastic to send your girlfriends overseas just to save you money, it may be worth considering the impact they do have on your expenditure. Could your friends be a real part of the reason you're spending way too much on clothes?

PUTTING YOUR MONEY TO WORK

I found it amusing when someone called me an investor just because I told them that I had invested money in a managed fund. I hardly thought of myself that way, because you think of an investor as some guy doing deals in a big stockbroking firm or something. All I did was take £500 and put this into a managed fund and then add £50 each month. It was really easy and I don't do anything, apart from checking the statement when it comes in the mail at the end of the financial year. **Anne, 29**

If you're still at the stage of struggling to keep on top of your bills, finding a lazy £50 to put away each month like Anne did might sound like a pipe dream. But you can get yourself into a position to do it, and it's definitely worthwhile.

If you put £50 a month into a managed fund earning, say, 6% interest a year, you would have £8,200 after 10 years. That's £2,200 more than the £6,000 you actually put away, thanks to compound interest. It's one smart way of making your money work for you.

Here are some sure-fire strategies to help you find that £50 every month to stash away in a savings account without compromising your lifestyle.

TIPS TO HELP GET YOU STARTED

1. Cut back on one coffee a day and only buy lunch three days a week and you could save as much as £750 a year.

2. Start your own movie club. We all love the movies so as well buying discounted cinema tickets, why not start a monthly DVD or video club? Use the same principles as a book club or gourmet club and share takeaway while watching the movie. Ask everyone to put in and you'll pay around £5 for the night, instead of £15 for a movie and a meal out.

3. Prepay your mobile phone bills. It's a great way to keep a check on how much you spend.

4. Be particular about ATMs. Withdraw money only from your own bank's ATMs. Ten withdrawals from other ATMs will cost at least £17.50 a month unnecessarily.

5. Carry minimum cash in your wallet. That way, you won't be tempted to spend.

6. Take out your loose change at the end of each day and drop it in a piggybank. You'll be surprised how much you can save with no noticeable impact on your spending.

7. Limit your credit card debt to a level you are able to pay off each month. And no matter how many times your bank encourages you to increase your limit, don't.

8. Get into the habit of walking. Save money that would otherwise go on public transport and cabs, and get fit.

9. Start a gourmet or book club. You'll have a lot of fun and save a wad of cash. Designate one night each month for a chance to catch up and gossip with girlfriends at each other's places.

10. Visit eBay and learn to shop online. If you buy wisely you can save a heap: remember Mary and her £9 designer shoes in Chapter Four.

11. Choose BYO over licensed restaurants. A little planning before your evening starts will mean painless savings, particularly if you are going with a large group where in a licensed venue the alcohol can cost at least as much as the food bill or more.

12. Only buy on sale. Adopt this habit from today. You can buy just about anything at a discount, if you just shop around. Did you know that many big shops (for instance, Peter Jones, John Lewis and Argos) will match competitors' prices at any time? You just have

to call around to find the best deal and then ask how much the chain will beat it by or whether they'll match it. You'll be surprised how quickly you start to think friends who pay the retail price of anything are crazy!

13. Get on the mailing list of your favourite designer and you'll find out ahead of the general public when their sales are on.

14. Opt for less flash beauty products. Consumer surveys have repeatedly shown that the Nivea, Ponds and Olay ranges offer the same benefits as the more glamorous brands, so don't be sucked in by the glossy ads, shop around and save.

15. Buy cheap theatre tickets on the internet, as long as you don't mind waiting till the end of a performance's run. Check a week or two before the end of season for last-minute deals.

16. Visit your local library if you're a keen reader. The books are up-to-date and free.

17. Don't forget internet auctions. There are some good and reputable online auction sites (for instance, www.ebay.co.uk and www.ebid.co.uk)

where you can buy anything from new computer equipment to secondhand furniture. Remember to set yourself a limit before you place a bid — and stick to it.

18. Write down your goals. Put them somewhere prominent to remind you why you are saving. This could be in your wallet, or as a screen saver, or written down in your diary at the start of each week. Tell your friends and family so everyone can support you.

Try at least five of these tips for one month and see how much you save. You'll soon be a convert.

CHAPTER EIGHT

CUTTING DOWN THE BIG TICKETS

So, day to day you're making a whole lot of small changes that are making a big difference. But what about those whacking great expenses like cars, weddings and travel? By being savvy you can save on these big-ticket expenses too.

A GIRL'S GOTTA HAVE WHEELS

Having your own car signals freedom. No more asking for rides from parents and friends. Or, worse still, after a great night out, being forced to stand around street corners trying to hail a cab.

Did you know most people choose a car based on the influence of parents, friends and boyfriends? For example, if your parents drove a Toyota, you may be swayed to do the same. Then again, you may opt for something you think reflects more of your own personality: sporty and fun, like a Honda Civic or Mazda MX5. If you want something on the conservative side you may prefer a classic saloon car. Or something funky like a BMW Mini. If you want a little more adventure a small 4WD is perfect. The bottom line is you need to pick a car that suits your lifestyle and budget.

But before we get to the nuts and bolts, what about the following for must-haves in a girl's dream car of the future:

- The obvious — more mirrors, please
- Automatic lipstick applicator
- 'Single male' detector. Detects the nearby males of your choice once you input your preferred stats, i.e. tall, dark and handsome with a red sports car
- Built-in steamer for pressing clothes
- Self-cleaning car, similar to self-cleaning oven
- A portable hairdryer that runs off the cigarette-lighter, or better still, a hair straightener. (I know a girl who actually asks cab drivers if she can plug her straightener into the cab cigarette-lighter socket to do her hair on the way.)
- Driver's seat massage feature
- Three sizes of cup holders for small/medium/large

skinny cappuccinos (depending on how late you
stayed up partying the night before)
- More colour choices inside and outside of the car,
or better yet, car seat covers you can change at the
flick of a switch to match your outfits
- More boot space for all the shopping bags

Now, back to what's actually out there ...

The consensus for how much you should pay for a
secondhand car is about £2,500. This is enough to get
you into some cool wheels and avoid a lemon. That's not
to say you can't buy a good car for under £2,500. It just
will take more work and research and you will be looking
at a car that is older and has more mileage.

While we love our wheels, there are ongoing expenses
that you will need to consider each year. If you live in a
city and work reasonably nearby, you may find that it is
truly more economical for you to take cabs and use public
transport when you consider all the costs associated with
owning a car.

When Amanda added it all up, catching public transport
was the only way to go. An environmentally conscious
employer was a big contributing factor in her decision.

I actually estimated what a car would cost me. I found the cost was
ridiculous when I compared it with public transport costs. When I did the
sums I included road tax, petrol, depreciation and general maintenance

and saw it was going to cost around £40 – £50 a week! This is after I had paid for the car. These additional costs would be ongoing, so catching public transport was much cheaper. I'm a bit of an environmentalist as well, so I do believe in catching public transport. I live in the inner city and generally getting around is fairly easy.

In my previous job I did have a company car and when I started this job with a local council I was entitled to a company car but I didn't take it, so they gave me an additional £3,000 a year as part of my salary package. The council is great because they are trying to encourage people to take public transport. Another incentive was they would pay for half of my weekly travel ticket.

So I take cabs or public transport to work. The council also provides access to a number of company cars for meetings during the day. The only thing is you don't take the car home at night. **Amanda, 26**

For Amanda getting by without a car is easy, but what about the rest of us who rely on our wheels? Let's look at some of the costs associated with owning a car. The biggies are:

- Road tax
- Compulsory third party insurance
- Comprehensive insurance
- Petrol
- Repairs and maintenance (and an annual MOT test if your car is more than 3 years old)
- Parking fees and tolls
- Depreciation

Road tax

Road tax is compulsory and can be bought for either six months (£93.50) or twelve (£170.00). To get your tax disc (which you must display on the inside of your windscreen) you must have a valid MOT certificate and a current insurance document.

Compulsory third party insurance

This is required by law in the UK and is mandatory when you tax your vehicle. CTP insurance covers everyone involved in a motor vehicle accident, except the driver who caused the accident, for costs that result from the accident.

Comprehensive insurance

You'd be mad not to have this if you can't afford to repair (or even lose) your car following an accident that you cause. It can be costly, but there are some great sites on the web that offer reduced premiums. They also offer flexible payment plans. Visit: www.churchill.com, www.ukcarinsurancedirectory.co.uk or www.diamond.co.uk. I saved more than £200 on my annual car insurance this way. If you have more than one car, the savings are even better.

Easy payment options such as monthly instalments are available, rather than paying one large annual bill (although it usually costs more to pay in instalments). In the past my car insurance was due in December and I found the cost on top of Christmas bills quite stressful. Now I opt to pay it twice a year and that has taken the pressure off.

Liz found out how worthwhile it was to shop around for insurance:

I found a massive difference in costs for my car insurance between different companies. I was amazed. I just thought I'd take a quick glance at it, because I figured they'd all be about the same. In the end, I spent 20 minutes on a website and about 40 minutes ringing around different companies, and it was so worth it.

I'm a late starter when it comes to driving – even though I'm 32 I only got my licence 18 months ago. I've only been driving for 6 months, which makes insurance much more expensive. I was looking for two different kinds of insurance – first up, Third Party Only. You need this to tax a car, and it pays for any damage you cause to other people with your car. The highest quote I got was £470, and the lowest was £425, so I saved a little bit there.

I also wanted to find out about general insurance for my car – if it got stolen or hit by an uninsured driver or damaged by a falling tree or whatever. I really didn't have a lot of money to buy the car in the first place, and I didn't want to go into debt over it because I'm trying to save for a house deposit, so I only spent £1,750 buying it. (I did a bit of research beforehand, to make sure I got something reliable – especially important when you have to buy an older car – and it paid off. The car is really reliable.)

Anyway, the quotes for comprehensive insurance – the kind that covers just about anything that could happen to it – were so different. The highest was £2,400 a year and the lowest was £1,150. Less than half! Maybe the first company (one of the biggies) stays in business because people don't check out other options. But even £1,150 was too much for a £1,750 car. Then I found another option.

The lowest of those quotes above came from a mob called Diamond. I just came across them in the phonebook when I was making a list for the ring-around. I'd never heard of them and thought they might be dodgy because of that, but I figured it wouldn't hurt to call. I looked into it and they turned out to be totally legit. It's just that they specialise in insuring women. (I should add that they do insure cars that are shared with a man, or regularly driven by one.) Women tend to have fewer accidents, and that keeps their costs down. And the company doesn't seem to spend money marketing itself.

They offered a kind of insurance that not every company offered, and it gave me what I needed at a price I could live with. It's called Third Party, Fire and Theft, and it covers me for damage I might do to other people's property, plus damage from fire, lightning, theft and attempted theft. It cost me £150 the first year (less this year). Other companies that did offer this insurance were all asking for much more.

So I got most of what I need (although I do still get very nervous when a storm is predicted, because I don't have insurance for that and I don't have a garage), and I saved hundreds of pounds. What I learned from all this was to shop around and look beyond the big companies you see advertised on TV. **Liz, 32**

Petrol

Don't forget that certain petrol stations are much cheaper than others. I have found that the petrol stations attached to the supermarkets are often the cheapest. Most offer some kind of loyalty points and these get to be worth quite a lot after a while — I saved £25 on my shopping bill at Sainsbury's through the Nectar card loyalty system.

Repairs and maintenance

This one is a little tricky and the best recommendation would be to ask your friends and family if they know a reputable mechanic. It is sad but true: if you're not careful you could end up paying for expenses that were really unnecessary, particularly if you're a young woman who is vulnerable and doesn't know anything about cars. But even couples can get caught out.

After saving £4,000 of their own money, Sally and her fiancé Robert bought a new car. They borrowed the extra £5,500 from a building society. They were also looking to buy a home and had shopped around and were happy with the lender. The agent offered them a good deal on the interest repayments.

There is nothing like owning a new car and so they were ecstatic when the keys were handed over. They felt pressured into agreeing when the car salesman said they must have the car serviced at his dealership, but because it was a new car they thought they wouldn't rack up any large expenses. The first and second time they had the car serviced they were charged £250 a visit. On the third visit they were charged £500 for a service on a car that was only 18 months old.

I didn't speak to Robert for a week. I had said to him earlier that we were paying too much and found out that if I had taken it to a normal registered mechanic for a service, it would have been a fraction of the cost. **Sally, 32**

Don't forget, we women have great instincts and if you feel uncomfortable or in any way patronised, just walk straight out. Lisa says she wishes she'd done just that. After continual disappointment with her mechanic's 'nit-picking' she finally decided to take her business elsewhere:

I felt extremely ill at ease each time I took my car to a local mechanic. I decided that this would be the last time as some of the charges were totally unnecessary. Get this, among other things he said my number plate was 'scratched and not straight enough'!

Every time I went he would pick on things that I felt were unjustified. I started to ask my female friends if they knew a good mechanic. Sure enough I got a recommendation from a friend and I'm so glad I made the change. The new mechanic is very approachable and friendly and I don't feel he is cheating me. He didn't even mention my number plate when I went for my MOT! **Lisa, 31**

Parking and tolls

Many car parks within shopping centres offer the first two hours free. Let's face it, no respectable girl is going to get her shopping done in less than two hours, so be prepared to pay the hourly fees thereafter. You're still far better to be in a car park than out on the street copping a hefty parking fine.

If you're going to land yourself parking fines, you may as well just save time and tear up £50 bills before you leave home.

After considering all the expenses, if you're still in the market for a car, here's what to look for:

A car-buying checklist

- Never buy a car from a salesman with a 'trust-me' attitude. Remember your instincts.
- Shop with a friend. A male friend would be ideal. (The world should have progressed by now for this not to be necessary but, sadly, it still is.)
- Depending on your job and your lifestyle you could spend many hours a week in your car, so make sure you pick a car to suit your lifestyle.
- Safety is paramount — if possible, buy a car with the three A's: Airbags, ABS brakes and air conditioning (comfort's pretty important too!).
- Take the car for a thorough test drive.
- Look out for rust or botchy paint jobs.

- Avoid cars that are 'gas guzzlers'. If you don't you'll find that petrol quickly becomes a major expense in your weekly budget.

There are some great sites around designed to take care of some of the hard work. You'll find used car values and new car prices, and reviews of various models. Check these websites:

- www.carprices.co.uk
- www.glass.co.uk
- www.parkers.co.uk
- www.wisebuyers.co.uk

Once you have found a car to your liking, have the vehicle inspected by your local motoring association, such as the AA or the RAC. It might seem pricey but this is not the time to skimp – the inspection report can save you wasting thousands on a dud.

If you plan to borrow to buy a car, shop around to get the best deal on interest payments. Don't hesitate to apply to banks and building societies if they come out ahead, even if you're not already a customer.

Consider buying a car at auction. I did this and saved more than £1,500 on the price of buying it privately. I did have my husband, who is good with cars, to give advice, which was important because when you buy at auction you don't get a warranty.

Make sure the car has its entire service history and logbooks. This will tell you whether or not it has been well maintained.

It sounds obvious, but when you're standing in front of a cute car with a cheque in your hand you can forget the basics, so it's worth a reminder: if possible, avoid cars with high mileage.

THE MOBILE PHONE

Not for one minute am I going to suggest that you consider life without your mobile phone. That would be like asking you to abandon one of your trusted friends. But if you've never really looked at how much yours is costing, you should. You could be paying much more than you need to.

Which one is more expensive: a mobile call to a friend who lives locally, or a call to Europe? You sure about that? Okay, read on.

I couldn't believe it the other day when I got my phone bill for my landline. I really did a double take. I'd made a call to Berlin and I had spoken for 14 minutes. This call was listed on the bill charged at £2.55. Also listed was a call I'd made to the mobile of a friend who was at home at the time, a couple of suburbs away. I spoke to my friend on the phone for about 17 minutes and was charged £8.75 for this. It was cheaper for me to call a land-line several hundred miles away than to call a mobile number a few miles away!

After that I decided to keep my calls to mobiles much shorter and really only use them for essential calls. **Kelly, 32**

With charges like this it's no wonder people find themselves spending a big chunk of each pay just on their phone bill.

Depending on your mobile phone provider, there are deals on offer that are worth their weight in gold, particularly if you choose one that has, say, free talk time. Lily explains:

I'm not technically minded and to be honest I only got a mobile phone two years ago. I was really confused by some of the deals.

[Aren't we all! For an industry that is all about communicating, the information they put out is incredibly detailed.]

And some of my friends were saying I should sign up to a plan. But I didn't want to go on a plan and be hooked into something I didn't understand. In the end I just settled on a re-charge card.

I charge it once every two months with £25 worth of credit. I also have free Vodafone-to-Vodafone minutes: when I re-charge I get three-and-a-half hours free talk time to another Vodafone mobile. A couple of my girlfriends use Vodafone too, so it works out really well. I don't know why more people don't get together with their friends and take advantage of this option.

I do text as well, sometimes more than I phone, mainly because I find it less intrusive and my friends can just check their text messages when it suits them.

I also still have a landline. I have been tempted to cancel it but I decided not to because I have family living in the country and they tend to call at night when I'm home, so if I keep the landline it costs them less. **Lily, 26**

Pre-paid works for Lily, but locking into a plan with lots of pre-paid minutes can be a good idea if you are racking up big phone bills each month, as Jennifer found:

I took up the payment option to have a bill that included 100 minutes of pre-paid calls each month. I took this out when I was living out of town because my bills were around £70 a month.

I'm not locked into any really long-term contract and I like that. I move house a lot and I don't want to keep getting a new number each time I move, like I would with a landline. My mobile number stays constant.

I pay £29.99 a month, which would be a bad deal if I ever used less phone time than this – but I never do. So in the end I'm making the same number of calls and saving about £480 a year. **Jennifer, 24**

Ring tones: why you may want to tune out

While it's great to have your own ring tone, just watch out for the charges. You are an individual and you want your phone to reflect this. That makes sense. The way your phone looks, feels and sounds can be a reflection of your personality. But getting caught up in the hype of having the latest hit on your phone each week can cost a tidy sum. If you think that the charges are not significant or if you're not sure how much you're spending this way, take a good look at your next phone bill. They are really popular but they're not cheap (and you need to keep changing your ring-tone to be trendy!)

Six tips to reduce your phone bills

Choose a phone payment to suit your profile. For example, prepaid is the best value for occasional users, while heavy users are better off with a contract or a plan with pre-paid minutes because the calls are cheaper. You'll also need to establish whether you're more of a text messager rather than a frequent caller, and shop around accordingly.

Don't overlook voicemail retrieval and deposit costs. Leaving and picking up messages can cost you eight to 10 pence per 30 seconds. So it's costing you money to leave a message and also for your caller to retrieve it. But some plans offer free voicemail and retrieval. If yours doesn't, shop around.

Don't forget the free talk time within networks. This is great if you have friends, your boyfriend or family with whom you are constantly in touch and can organise to be on compatible networks.

The best place to start when looking for a phone and a contract are the mobile phone shops like the Carphone Warehouse. Thay all produce a leaflet comparing all the different costs and options with different providers. The Consumer Association website www.which.net also can advise on the best phone plan for you. There is a small membership fee, £23.25 a quarter (after a 30-day free trial) to access the information. This could be money well spent, since the fee lets you search not just on phone info but on almost every consumer item imaginable. The site www.studentlife.com/life/telephone/mobile.htm also offers useful tips and www.half.co.uk lists the latestoffers with comparisons.

Try wherever possible to use a landline. If you know that you'll be home or back in the office soon then wait to make those non-urgent calls.

Check your phone bill. Contact your provider if you see any suspicious charges.

THE WORLD IS YOUR OYSTER

Travel is a dream that motivates many people. The years of study are over and you are now working and earning your own money. You have the world at your feet. This was certainly how I felt in my early 20s, with a strong desire to spread my wings and find adventure.

Tina is currently planning her own adventure. She and her boyfriend are saving together, and are well on their way to achieving their goal. She has found that cutting back on those small daily expenses — a coffee here, takeaway there — has really made a big difference. And she just has to think of her planned six-week holiday in India to stay focused.

Going overseas is the big motivator for my saving. I have budgeted to spend only £35 through the week on top of the £25 I put aside for my transport costs. I have been doing this for the last six months or so. But don't worry, I'm not starving myself! I bring food to work each day from our weekly grocery shopping. It also helps that there aren't many places to go for lunch near my office so I don't feel like I'm missing out. It's an effort to get into town to shop at lunchtime, so it's not too much of a temptation.

My boyfriend and I are saving together. Our aim is to have about £4,000 between us after 12 months' saving. We are at the halfway mark now and so far we are on track.

If I really need anything, for instance clothes, I do try to find it at a discount or wait until the sales. I'd rather buy one thing I really love and wear it a lot than buy a few cheaper things that I don't like as much. I know that I will pick up some nice things when I'm in India. So it's really not that hard to be tempted. I wish my travel plans were as organised as my budget! **Tina, 25**

Booking travel online

Years ago the only way to book travel was through a travel agency. The agent would take your booking details, recommend places to visit and stay, and seek out the best deals for you. Their job was to take all the hard work out for the traveller. Things didn't always go as planned, but at least you had a bricks-and-mortar business to go to if something went wrong.

Now most people will do at least some of their travel booking online. Doing it this way has many advantages:

you can do it in the privacy of your own home any time that suits, and cutting out the middle step often means you save money. Trawling through hundreds of web pages can be a little mind-numbing, though, so a recommendation is always a good place to start.

And a little caution goes a long way with online travel shopping, particularly if you are booking and paying for something that is on the other side of the world. Lots of people make bookings online and have no dramas whatsoever. But some internet sites leave a little to be desired, as one couple travelling to Paris found.

Aiming to book a museum pass ahead of their arrival, to save time and money, they found what they thought was a reputable site (museums-of-paris.com) and ordered and paid for two three-day museum passes, for a total charge of 88 euros (about £65).

They received an email confirmation saying the passes would be waiting at their hotel. But the passes never arrived. There was a phone number on the confirmation email and, since they didn't speak French, they asked their hotel receptionist to call it and check. She tried several times but the number rang out every time. They began to realise they had fallen for a scam.

Back home they found that their credit card had been debited the full amount. When they tried to email the address provided for queries, their email bounced back. They phoned the Paris number again, but of course it still rang out.

The lesson here is that anyone can fall victim to a scam but you can cut down the chances of it happening to you by making sure there is a phone number on the site you intend to book through, and calling it to see whether anyone answers before you start providing credit card details. The amount you spend on the call is insurance against losing much more of your hard-saved money. Another good tactic is to only buy from sites you can access through government tourism sites — they are likely to be the real deal.

Best travel websites

It almost goes without saying that there are plenty of great travel deals online. To help you start looking, here are a few tried and tested sites:

- www.hotels.com
- www.lastminute.co.uk
- www.travelocity.co.uk
- www.cheapflights.co.uk
- www.expedia.co.uk
- www.hotelroomsplus.com
- www.cheapaccommodation.com
- www.fodors.com
- www.travelsupermarket.com
- www.bargainholidays.com
- www.travel-agents.org
- www.thefirstresort.com

For something a little bit different try:

· www.karenbrown.com
· www.cadoganguides.com

If Asia is your thing, then this site is worth a visit:

· www.elephantguide.com/home.htm

Lonely Planet's series of books cover most countries. They offer insight into the places to stay and eat. They are particularly good if you're on a budget. See www.lonelyplanet.com for more information.

The UK Government issues important travel and insurance tips, including info aimed at female travellers. For the latest advice and warnings on trouble spots visit www.fco.gov.uk/travel (FCO stands for the Foreign and Commonwealth Office, a branch of the Government).

Travel insurance

Don't even think about going overseas without travel insurance. We take a lot for granted when we're in our own country, but you can't do that elsewhere. If you're travelling in a foreign country and you lose your luggage, get ill or have money or goods stolen, your whole holiday can be ruined. But if you have travel insurance you can get help at the time and replace any remaining items once you're home.

And then there are medical emergencies to consider. An emergency hospital visit is not free in the USA or elsewhere in the way that it is in the UK. Even simple problems can cost you thousands of pounds if you're not insured.

Andie is a travel agent who had always recommended travel insurance to her clients, and one day found out just how useful it was:

A few years ago I was in San Francisco Airport waiting for my baggage to come off the carousel. As the bags came out everyone started noticing items that had obviously come from someone's damaged luggage. We were all sniggering, until I noticed a familiar Mickey Mouse moneybox and saw it was broken. I thought 'Wait a minute, that looks like the one I bought for my nephew.' Slowly the other items came around and of course I realised they were my possessions, my clothes and more gifts for my family back home. I was so embarrassed. I tried not to make it obvious, but I felt like crying.

I then saw my luggage and it was ripped in half. I picked up the pieces and tried to pick up all my possessions as well. I went over to the United Airlines baggage counter and proceeded to tell my story. I was half laughing and half crying.

I've always had travel insurance, but never had to use it until that day. I knew they could not reimburse me on the spot but they were very good and gave me a statement, acknowledging that my bag was damaged and that I had lost things that were not on the carousel.

I made sure to take a note of everything I lost. This was important as I knew by the time I got back to London I would have forgotten. When I got home I obtained a claim form and completed it accordingly. Luckily, I still had the receipts for the gifts and I sent them in with the form. I also kept a photocopy for myself.

A few weeks later I got a cheque covering everything I'd lost. Luckily it was my sports bag that had ripped, not my main bag so it was a relatively small amount – around £175. But that was a lot more than the cost of the insurance. **Andie, 34**

If you can't afford travel insurance, then you can't afford to travel.

Here are a couple of useful sites to start you shopping around:
- www.insureandgo.com
- www.cheaptravelinsurance.net
- www.travel-insurance-online.com

UNIVERSITY FEES AND STUDENT LOANS

A little while ago, a leading breakfast radio show ran interviews with a group of students about the impact of university fees and how they thought their student loan debt would affect their future. Most believed that by age 30 they would be earning £75,000 a year and have two cars. Some even thought they would be retired by then.

Most of those interviewed were around 18. They're certainly allowed to have big dreams, but during the show callers rang in to let them know that the reality was very different. One 30-year-old who called in was a junior solicitor, earning around £29,000 a year and still owing £12,000 in student loan fees. Another, aged 30, owned a medical company and was married with two kids. He was indeed earning £75,000 a year, but he worked a 70-hour week and sacrificed a lot for his business. Another caller was a fashion student who after six years' study realised her average earning potential was just £22,000 a year.

The big money doesn't necessarily follow once you have completed your degree. It may come later with experience under your belt. In the meantime you have that student loan debt. So what are the options?

Pay now or pay later? Why it may make sense to defer

Did you know that your student loans do not attract a real interest rate? Instead, the interest on the debt is set to match the rate of inflation, which is currently about 2.1%. Savings in the right sort of account will earn you double this. So why would you pay your student loan costs if you are studying full-time? You have the option of deferring loan payments until you are in the workforce, and it makes sense to do this so you don't have the added pressure of trying to pay your debt while studying.

Caroline decided she would defer her student loan payments and put savings from the money she earns in her part-time job into a term deposit earning 5.5%.

I'll finish my law degree next year and will have a student loan debt of £12,500. Before I enrolled at university my parents and I discussed whether they should pay for it up front. But since there is basically no interest fee, it made sense to leave it until I was earning a decent wage. I didn't want to put so much financial pressure on my parents.

I work in a department store one or two days a week. When I started I set up a term deposit and have half my pay put into this account. I earn around 5.5% interest and I don't touch this money as I want to save for a car. When I get a job in law in about two years, I will start my student loan repayments. **Caroline, 26**

Deferring is often also the best option if you have other debt. For instance, Sue has just finished a law degree and owes £12,500 on her student loan. She also has a £1,000 credit card debt and savings of around £3,000. She recently started a new job. She asked me for advice on the best plan for her money.

As I told Sue, she should pay off her credit card debt completely and maybe keep the card for emergencies. But she doesn't need to worry about paying off the student loan for now, because it's essentially a non-interest generating debt. There is no urgency to pay off this debt as there is with a credit card.

But deferring the debt doesn't mean avoiding it. And you will feel the effects of making the compulsory repayments once you start work. Josephine opted to defer and she is now working and has her payments taken out of her salary. Even after a pay-rise, she still finds she has to keep an eye on her spending.

When I enrolled at university to do a Bachelor of Media Law I opted to pay all my uni costs by taking out a student loan. It would have been great to have the money to pay my fees then, but I didn't, so it wasn't an option. As soon as I got a job I started making the mandatory contributions through my pay. I had incurred a £12,500 debt.

I pay my contributions straight after my salary goes into my account. Once the student loan payments are taken out, and on top of that income tax and pension payments, there is not much left. Even though I got a £2,000 pay increase after my three-month review, once everything was taken out I basically got only £85 extra a month. What I did do was put £50 out of the £85 I got into an interest-bearing savings account because I want to travel. I hope to have my student debt paid off within the next two years. **Josephine, 27**

Getting your employer to pay

Of course, if your employer pays you don't have to worry about student fees and loans at all — as long as you perform well. Sylvia's employer was happy to support her studies, with a few conditions attached.

I had been in the workforce for about eight years when I decided to go back to university to finish my degree. I decided to do it part time because I have a full-time job with a large finance company. Our company has a policy that if you are doing a course that is in the same field of work then they will reimburse the fees and help with a small amount each month towards other costs. My finance degree fits the criteria so there was no problem getting my employer to pay.

They agreed to reimburse my university and textbook fees on the proviso that I pass each subject. If I didn't pass the subjects, they would not reimburse me, and if I decide to leave the company before I finish my degree, I have to pay back the last year's fee my employer reimbursed.

I'm now in my third year. It is fantastic that the company has reimbursed me because it made it easier, but on the other side there is a lot of pressure to pass each subject. Still, it's great they are willing to do it. University is so expensive and when you're working and paying off a mortgage, this helps so much. **Sylvia, 32.**

If you work for a large organisation then your HR department will be aware of the policy on sponsoring you through university. If your company has a good intranet it might be listed on it. In some organisations reimbursement is agreed to at the manager's discretion (if you're seen as a great asset to the company this may be part of the incentive program they offer you in order to keep you loyal). If you work for a smaller organisation, it will probably be harder to arrange sponsorship, but check with your immediate boss to find out. If you think you might be interested in further study at some point and you are in the process of interviewing for a new job, ask about the policy on training and fees.

Another option to pay for uni

Savvy girl Veronica bought a three-bedroom house in order to supplement her uni fees. She made this clever

move with money she had saved and thanks to some help from her mother:

I bought the house when I was 20, largely due to the influence and advice of my mum. I was studying at university and there was an opportunity to buy a property and rent the rooms out to other students. I had some savings from working part-time. With that and some money I borrowed from my family, I had enough for a deposit, so I applied for a loan. The house had three bedrooms, so I had two friends renting with me to pay the mortgage and I was able to live rent-free.

I still have the property and I rent it out. I am so glad I did it back then because now that I am working I do spend a lot. I love clothes and shoes. I also spend about £35 travelling to and from work; sometimes I'm running late and I'll get cabs. I also buy my lunch every day and I do have a very busy social life.

This doesn't worry me so much because I know I have a house. I believe I'm in a better position than my girlfriends because I have savings (in a managed fund) and the house. I can spend, knowing that I have all that behind me. Some of my friends spend up and don't have anything. We're planning a trip to Greece in two months and for me the money this will cost is no problem. I really enjoy my life; I can take trips, buy nice clothes. I did get carried away with my credit card and racked up £3,250. I knew I was going too far and now I've put the card away and I have a payment plan. I've paid half. I'll have the rest paid in three months. **Veronica, 28**

While this is a little bold, even unusual, it has proved to be a great move for Veronica. Today she enjoys the fruits of her savings and is able to spend on the things she loves. (Yes, she has gone a little overboard on her credit card and she could use the money in her managed fund to pay off her debt, but given that she is on track to have it paid off within three months, she's probably better off leaving that investment alone.) If your parents are prepared to pay for your university fees, then why not consider using this money for a deposit on a house in which you can have boarders?

WEDDING BELLS, WEDDING BILLS

The time has come when your treasured girlfriends no longer take centre stage in your life. You don't say 'I' any more. It's been replaced by 'we': 'We are going there', 'We are looking at a place to live', 'We did this', 'We did that', 'We are getting married'.

Fabulous. But getting married is stressful. I almost fell off my chair when I read recently that the average wedding costs between £8,000 and £15,000. No wonder it's a strain for the couple and their families.

I have never met a bride whose skin hasn't broken out on the day of the wedding or at the very least who hasn't lost sleep over the cost and the arrangements. It'll happen to you, too, unless you plan to elope. But if your intention is to have a wedding with family and friends, you can minimise the stress by starting to plan as far ahead as possible.

In terms of the basics, as soon as you mention weddings you can just add an extra zero to the cost of everything. The cake, dress and venue are all big money-spinners for suppliers.

Sandra and Greg were very aware of the way costs could spiral out of control, so they came up with a plan to avoid that happening:

We probably did things the opposite of most couples, because we had already bought our home and were living together for three years before we decided to get married.

We figured the amount we could save while we were young and earning good money was well spent towards our first home. Also we didn't have family to fall back on so having our wedding paid for by parents was not an option.

We were really happy that we reached our goal and that was to buy our home. Then when we decided we wanted to get married, I didn't find the extra saving hard at all. Buying a house – that really teaches you how to save.

The first thing I did was put a budget together on an Excel spreadsheet. I put down a figure of £8,000, which was the upper limit we wanted to spend. I listed all the costs associated with the wedding. Each time I paid for something or got a quote I would put this on the spreadsheet and it would calculate how much I had left. I found this helped enormously.

I limited the amount I wanted to spend on my dress to £800. A friend is a makeup and hair stylist and she did the makeup for me and my bridesmaids. I spent my lunchtimes looking at ideas from websites, and at invitations. In the end I did the invitations myself and this saved around

£600. Most of the money we spent went on the reception. We had 120 guests. Quite a few had travelled across the globe to join us, so we wanted a venue with great food and atmosphere.

My advice to any bride is to be realistic about the cost. It will be very expensive, particularly if you are after a traditional wedding with lots of guests. As soon as you tell a supplier that you are getting married they mark up everything by 100%, whether it's the cake, the dress or hair.

Buy or borrow some bridal magazines for ideas. Be careful about additional charges from photographers – you may think that you have paid for the photos of your wedding, only to find each print is an extra cost. Speak to your friends who have been married. Use word of mouth, particularly for florists, makeup and hair, as you really don't want to be stressed about the way you look or feel on the day. Also, you don't want to feel as though you've been ripped off. I know it's hard, but try not to make decisions based on emotions. **Sandra, 30**

Would you have your wedding sponsored?

This story may seem a little bizarre, but it worked for one couple (in the USA admittedly!). Having decided it was time to get married, they didn't want to ask their parents for the money and didn't have enough themselves, so they came up with an innovative idea: why not have their wedding sponsored?

They approached local businesses and asked if they would like to donate their goods or services to their wedding. In return they would promote the sponsors to the 180 guests.

It turned out that local businesses were only too willing to help. The only thing the couple ended up paying for was the reception and the bride's wedding dress — US$7,000 worth. The total value of everything else, which was donated, was US$40,000. All the sponsors were thanked and promoted throughout the event. Okay, okay, maybe it's not for you, but you have to give them 10 points for originality and making it a success.

Over the last four years I have seen three of my sisters marry. Naturally, there were moments of frustration and anxiety, but what got them through was their careful planning. There are some great websites to get you started. One I particularly like is www.ezweddingplanner.com. It's amazing — I wish I'd had something like this when I got married. It is so comprehensive; everything from protocol to vows. For starters there is a budget page. This covers every little expense, everything you could possibly imagine, and it's easy to use. The wedding planner itself will help you keep track of all the must-do details leading up to your wedding date. You can add your own 'To Do's' as well. You'll receive an email of your planned items as they become due, so you don't forget anything. Having recently married, my sister Rhonda shares her experiences:

I know you should be over the moon when your partner asks you to marry, but as I mentioned earlier [in Chapter Two] I was really scared, because we didn't own anything at the time. You have this picture in your mind of couples saving together to buy their house and car. We didn't have any of this when we decided to get married.

We had to wait almost three years after Michael proposed, because we had to get our act together. We bought our two-bedroom unit six months before we were due to marry but even after we bought it we kept up our routine of adding £175 a week into the account we'd used to save our deposit. In that six months we had saved several thousand pounds, and we both received tax refunds, which went straight into this account.

I figured the wedding was going to cost £10,000. Unfortunately we were short by £4,000, although we still had a little bit of time to keep saving. As timing would have it, we received some sad news that Michael's grandmother had passed away. We also found out that some money was left to him. The money was literally sent from heaven (although we would have preferred Nan to be at our wedding). We put this money straight into the savings account and did not touch it.

The best thing I found to help me keep on top of the wedding budget was this fabulous website: www.ezweddingplanner.com. I downloaded the wedding planner and put in the amount we had budgeted for. There is so much to shell out for before the wedding – deposits for this and that, the cake and reception. I was able to keep track of what was going out and how much I had left. I would also get reminders when payment was due and what I should be doing three months out, two months out, etc. It's really worthwhile having something like this. There is so much to think about, especially if you decide to have a big wedding.

We were fortunate that family members gave us cash as wedding presents. This almost paid for the reception and even though we spent a lot of money on the wedding, we still had £3,000 left. We would have been able to save the amount even without the help of Nan, but it really took the pressure off. She must have been smiling down from heaven.
Rhonda, 34

THE TO-DO LIST

Agree on a budget

The last thing you want to do with your future husband is start your married life fighting over the cost of your wedding. Unless your parents are going to pay for your wedding and money is of no concern you should agree how much you are prepared to spend.

Your idea of the perfect wedding may be to have 20 close friends and family celebrating in your backyard or 200 guests at a swanky hotel. No matter what you have in mind, agree on a figure and put everything into the budget planner.

Get real figures

Visiting sites such as the one mentioned above will help you keep within your wedding budget. For instance, let's say the budget for your wedding is £8,000. You can set up a spreadsheet, put this amount as the total and enter all the costs along the way. This will keep track of all your spending and help you stay within budget. Talking to friends who have recently been married will give you a realistic idea of your likely expenditure. My sisters have become experts and have saved their friends hundreds, perhaps thousands, of pounds.

Learn to compromise

Let's be honest here. If you're getting married then, like every couple, you've already learnt the art of compromising. Compromising in some areas of your big day can work wonders with your wedding budget, especially if it's tight.

You can save on some areas, and splash out on others. You may not want to skimp on your wedding dress, but you could save money by making your own invitations. There are some great software packages and websites to help you design an invitation. For example, any home or office printer can provide a professional finish if you have quality stationery paper to print on. Opting for finger food and a cocktail reception instead of a sit-down dinner means you can afford a fabulous venue instead of an average one. You get the idea.

£250

CHAPTER NINE

IT'S TRUE: MONEY MAKES MONEY

Once you have your money problems under control you need to know about investing. If that sounds scary, relax, it's not. Even if all you want to do is open a savings account and start a savings plan, you are ready to invest. But it often sounds much more complicated than that, and boring and intimidating to boot. And if you're still in your old mindset, it also sounds totally uncool. It's easy to get scared off.

I think a lot of finance stuff is directed at men, as opposed to young women. I'm not saying there is some big overt sexism going on here, but it does feel like you are in an arena where men know more about finance. Being able to identify with them would be good. **Alison, 27**

Take heart, Alison. A recent study looking into the number of individuals owning shares shows that about eleven million Britons own shares, either directly or indirectly through things such as managed funds, and many of these are women. So women are getting more involved — investing is no longer the sole domain of men. If you feel left out, don't forget that you may already own shares if you have a pension fund.

And shares are only one investment option. You can start off small to get used to the idea:

When I was younger my dad tried to tell me about saving, and how you should think about wealth generation. I didn't pay attention. I had this really negative attitude towards money and talking about money and blah, blah ... I just didn't like people who were concerned with money. But now that I am 25 and working I've started to realise that this negative attitude hindered me, and refusing to learn about it wasn't going to work either. I decided whether I like it or not, money is something you can't really avoid, so you might as well try to understand it. I actually called my dad a few months ago and told him I want to develop a savings plan.

Dad said 'I don't care what you do with the rest of your money, just get into the habit of putting some away.' So we opened a savings account. I now have 10% of my salary put into it each month. **Jane, 25**

Jane has made a great start with minimum effort. It's little steps like this that will set you on the path to really becoming savvy about investing.

Right now you are probably having a great time spending the money you work so hard for. But at some point as you get older you may look back and say 'What have I got to show for all my hard work?' That's what happened to Lisa.

From the moment I started working I wanted to travel. I have travelled just about every year for the past eight years. It wasn't until I reached the age of 30 that I realised I had nothing to show for my years of working. I didn't own a car and I've been renting since I left home. You might say that 30 was a turning point for me because it was then that I got a little nervous about the future and what I've got to rely on. I know I have my pension fund, but from what I keep hearing I wonder if that's going to be enough. Will I be able to keep travelling when I retire? This is something I'm really passionate about.

I've been renting for so long I thought it was time to start saving for a place of my own. The first thing I did was open an interest-earning savings account. I want to use this money for a deposit on a unit. I have £250 taken out of my pay each month.

I hadn't been in a long-term relationship for over five years and that was another factor in wanting something secure for myself. In about six months I'll start looking for my own place. A few months back I met a guy and our relationship has really grown. He is really supportive of me saving money and my goals. I'd like to think he is the right one, but we'll just have to wait and see. Either way I'll have something that I can call my own. **Lisa, 32**

ARE YOU DESPERATE AND INDEBTED
OR READY TO INVEST?

Before we move ahead, a caution: if you are struggling to pay off your debts and losing sleep over them, then you are not ready to invest. Not yet anyway. Clear your debts first. On the other hand, if you have some money lying around, then read on. If you're stuck in the middle – in other words you've plateaued, you're covering your expenses but don't have much left over – use some of the tips from Chapter 7 to start saving so that you have money to invest.

Simply put, if you are thinking of investing and you are still paying off debts, then the answer is 'No'. Your priority has to be paying off your debts, then you will be able to start investing with a clear conscience.

TIME IS ON YOUR SIDE

You may not have considered this, but you are probably in your best earning years right now. If you are between 25 and 35 you are more likely to be single, in a well-paid job, and have minimal debts. Compare this to the next stage, when you may be married, have a mortgage and small children. Your budget will be stretched to cover many more expenses.

If you are single and in a well-paid job, this is the perfect time to get your head around investing and understand why it makes sense to start now. It was a lesson that I learned.

I caught the investing bug at the tender age of 24. This happened purely by coincidence and on reflection was a huge risk for me. Before you start you'll have to determine whether you are risk averse or a risk-taker. I discovered I am a risk-taker. (Today I'd like to say I take calculated risks.) I am glad that I am. If I hadn't been, I would not have bought my home and built up other investments.

When I was 24, I was given a 'hot share tip' by my brother. At the time gold shares were very hot, but choosing the right one was tricky. I didn't have a clue about investing, but I was interested. I handed £2,000 to my brother, who proceeded to invest the money in gold-mining shares. (Naivety, youth and stupidity is all I can think of when I recall these events. Never would I do that again.) I struck it big with the shares, but it was beginner's luck. My £2,000 very quickly became £4,000.

That was my first step on the road of investing. In the early days I thought myself a casual investor and only took a punt on recommendations from family and friends. I sold the gold shares; the value had reached a high of £6,000 then started dropping. I sold them when they were worth £4,000 and used this to invest in my first home. My money was now making money.

(It is important to note that while my first investment was a success, not all have been. Another gold-mining company that my husband and I had shares in went bankrupt and we lost all the money we had invested in it.)

Anyway, back to those early days. Life appeared to be wonderful. I was married, I had finally bought a home and I had a great job in the advertising industry. Having put the money into a house, my focus switched away from investing. Until the day I got retrenched.

Suddenly I had no job, a very large mortgage, and, I soon discovered, a baby on the way. Was I stressed? You bet! I decided to start my own consultancy, inspired by the entertainment maestro Walt Disney, who started Disneyland because no one would give him a job. It took several months to establish myself and it made me wish that I had some money to fall back on. I should have kept investing.

Luckily I had plenty of contacts and finally the work started to come through, enough to pay my bills. But the experience of having been retrenched left me shaken and I vowed to put some security behind me, in case I should find myself without work again.

My interest in the stockmarket increased rapidly and I started to read a lot and attend seminars through the stock exchange. I asked lots of questions and read books about investing in shares and property. Initially I did have a broker, but with the advent of online trading, I decided to do it myself. A few years later, I started an investment club with some friends, which has been fantastic. The girls are a great source of support and information. In a group we cover more ground than someone trying to do it on their own.

If times get tough again, it's reassuring to know I have built up a pool of resources.

Money makes money. That is not to say you have to be wealthy before you start investing, but investing can make you wealthy. Of course, there are risks involved. First, determine what sort of an investor you are; for example, are you risk averse or a risk-taker? You need to know in order to be comfortable with the choices you make.

To start with let's look at the four main areas for investing and the risks associated with them:

1. Cash or fixed-term deposits
2. Shares
3. Managed funds/Unit Trusts
4. Property

CASH OR FIXED-TERM DEPOSITS: 'THE UNTOUCHABLE SAVINGS'

My attitude towards saving I learnt from my dad, and that is to put money aside for the future and do what you want with the rest. From my fortnightly pay cheque I put money aside into a term deposit for a trip I'm planning, and what's left is money to spend for the week. More often than not I get to my next pay cheque with only £5 left in my wallet. But this is okay. I don't feel as though I've burnt all my money because I have put away that money into what I call my 'untouchable savings'.

I'm just starting out and this money will eventually go into some sort of investment and generate some income. **Rebecca, 27**

Cash or fixed-term deposits are very popular with young women. Probably because if you have a small nest-egg to start with they are easy to set up and you'll receive decent interest on the money you have invested. Compare this to having your money sitting in a regular bank account barely earning 0.25%.

One of the reasons cash or fixed-term deposits are popular is that they are generally low risk and easy to obtain. Most banks offer fixed-term deposits, returning around 2% to 2.5% for an investment of £5,000. The return depends on how much you have invested – the more you have invested, the higher the rate of return. The length of time your money is invested will also determine the interest you receive. The shortest available term is usually three months and the longest is a couple of years. To get the maximum interest from your investment, leave it for as long as possible. You can have the interest you earn added to your original amount and reinvest the total automatically, or you can choose to have the interest paid out to you at the end of each period. The fixed-term part of the deal means that you agree to leave your money there for that period; if you take it out earlier you won't get the full amount of interest.

Term deposits are great if you are unsure what to do with your money or if you are building up a specific amount (for instance, a target figure to use as a mortgage deposit). If the money is just sitting in your regular bank account the temptation to pull it out is always there. That's not to say accessing your money from a term deposit is difficult, it is not. It generally only takes a phone call and the money is transferred across into the day-to-day account of your choice, usually in a day or two.

But you don't have to have £5,000 to get these interest rates or even higher. Online banks are the best place to look for accounts that pay good interest but have very small minimum deposits or no minimums at all. ING Direct is an example, with an account called the Savings Account that pays 4.75% interest and has no minimum deposit and no bank fees. You do, though, need an everyday transaction account (i.e. an account with a bank that has regular branches) in order to transfer the money in and out. You can open the account online and the beauty of it is that the interest is calculated on your balance at the end of each day, and then added to your account at the end of each month.

Jenny found one of these online accounts very useful:

Some time ago, a friend recommended I put some money aside in a term deposit. It sounded like a good idea but I never had the time to get to the bank to fill out an application. Then I found that I could open an account online and earn the same amount of interest. I opened an account with ING Direct. It was really easy.

I have £200 a month taken from my salary and put into the account. Also, when I have some spare cash, I add to it. I like the fact that I can withdraw money when I really need it. I can do this by transferring the money online into my normal bank account. It's more flexible than a term deposit, but it's not as tempting as having a normal bank account because I don't have an ATM card to access the money. **Jenny, 29**

To find out more, start with:

- www.ingdirect.co.uk
- www.savings.infospot.com
- www.moneyexpert.com

A tax reminder
The interest you receive on banked money is classified as income so you will need to declare it come tax time.

SHARES: RESEARCH AND RISK CAN PAY OFF
I've mentioned the great experience I had in my investment club — our timing certainly helped. We started in the late 1990s, which just happened to be perfect timing. The sharemarket had been experiencing good times, with the value of shares rising and rising — what's called a bull market. Dotcoms and technology shares hadn't yet crashed and there was a lot of interest in shares.

As well, internet trading started. In the past you had to buy and sell shares through a broker at a charge of £30 or more a trade. Today you can still use a broker if you wish, but you can also do it yourself very simply online at a fraction of the cost.

That has made it worthwhile to buy a parcel of shares if you have as little as £150 saved up. Obviously, the more money you have to put into your purchase the more you might earn by selling them at a profit. But there are no guarantees with shares. In dire and extreme situations, shares that cost £10 each to buy might be worth just a few pence when you want to sell them.

The golden rule of share trading is: only invest what you can afford to lose.

That is a harsh reality, but shares are different from investments like term deposits, where you are guaranteed your initial investment back as well as the money you have earned on it. Another difference between share trading and other forms of investment, such as a managed fund, is that in such a fund someone else does the work for you. With share trading, even if you use a broker I strongly recommend learning about the market and keeping an eye on your shares.

So share trading is for you if you can live with risky investment and you're prepared to do some work. But let's go right back to the basics to make sure you understand the world you're thinking about entering ...

What is a share?

When you buy a share in a company, you become a shareholder who owns a part of that company. For example, I own shares in Royal Bank of Scotland. Each time I look at its grand old flagship building in Edinburgh, I think 'I own part of that company, even if it's only one brick!'.

What is a dividend?

When you own shares in a company you may receive a dividend. A dividend is like a 'reward' for investing in that company. It is usually paid twice a year. You may choose to have the dividend paid into your nominated bank account or you may choose to have it paid in shares in the company. That is called dividend reinvestment and it means that you end up with more shares without having to buy them. Some newer companies may not pay dividends until they become more firmly established.

Tax

Like any return from an investment, you will need to declare money you make from shares on your tax return. You can make money in two ways — a dividend or capital gains. If your shares pay a dividend you have to pay tax on that amount. But all dividends are paid net at the basic rate of tax before you get the money, and you get a statement telling you how much. You then only have to pay the difference between the tax percentage they've already taken out and your own personal tax level.

Capital gains is the name for the amount you make when you sell shares at a higher price than you paid for them. If you buy £500 worth and you sell them a year or two later for £750, your capital gain is £250. You will have to pay capital gains tax (CGT), although you do get a CGT allowance each year of £8,500. Any losses (capital loss) you incur that tax year can be offset against any gains you make.

Take time to educate yourself because while you are learning you have nothing to lose.

How do I decide what shares to buy?

You should only be dabbling in the stockmarket if you understand it. I followed this rule myself, and I'm glad I did. Before I bought anything I built up my knowledge and confidence. I spent a lot of time reading relevant books and newspaper articles and attending seminars, and I found I was genuinely interested in the sharemarket and investing. If you're not, if it all sounds too hard, then another form of investment is probably best for you (although there is the 'blue-chip' halfway step — see below).

Before you begin investing in shares, whether you go through a broker, do it yourself or start an investment club, get into the habit of reading the business section of the newspaper regularly. At the back of most business sections you'll find sharemarket tables. These list share prices for the previous business day. It gives you the last share price traded, plus a figure for the highest price paid and the lowest price paid for each share.

Follow a couple of specific shares for about a month — perhaps well-known companies such as the major banks, or even the company you work for, if it's listed. This will help you to understand how share prices fluctuate.

If you want to pursue it further, the London Stock Exchange (the LSE) is the best place to start. It puts out a handy little booklet for first-timers called 'How to Build a Portfolio'. The LSA website is www.londonstockexchange.com. www.moneyextra.com is another useful website that explains how the stockmarket works and how you can plan to get started on your portfolio — and maybe your fortune!

Education with a bonus

Several years ago I attended one of those Stock Exchange courses. I walked in and found a room full of men!

The first thing that came to my mind, given that I was already married, was: Where are my sisters and single girlfriends? For a minute I almost forgot why I was there.

Forget RSVP and other internet dating services. Say goodbye to expensive, smoky bars. Investment education sessions like this (not the shonky 'instant millionaire' type) are full of interesting men who are open to new things and committed to building financial security, just like you. These sessions are well worth attending for their own sake, but who knows, you may get more than you bargained for!

The blue-chip option – a halfway step

For those who like the idea of shares but not the research needed to really get on top of the stockmarket, a halfway step is to buy what are called blue-chip shares. These are shares in companies that have a good reputation for making profits, no matter whether the market is high or low, and they generally offer reliable growth over the long term. Though their dividend payments may be lower, they tend to be less risky than other, more volatile, shares. Think of them as 'the set and forget'. Examples of blue-chip companies are the major banks like RBS and Lloyds TSB, and resource giants like BP.

You already know more than you think

When it does come time to buy shares, a little bit of commonsense helps you to predict future trends. For example, let's take a look at a period in which a housing boom occurs. Ask yourself which companies are likely to profit from a housing boom. With more people borrowing more money, logically the banks will benefit, and this will be reflected in their share prices. This is just what happened recently. Another example is that during periods of strong economic growth and low unemployment people are likely to spend more. Who will benefit? The retail stores.

It's not always this simple, but a bit of commonsense still goes a long way.

Not-so-hot tips

Once you have 'come out' and let your friends and workmates know you're investing in shares you'll find many people are only too happy to talk about their investments. And while their intentions may be well meaning, they will often want to pass on a 'hot tip' that may not be so hot at the end of the trading day. My one word of advice is: caution. Sometimes 'hot tips' come good, but for the most part they don't.

I learned this the hard way. A colleague of mine who had been investing in the sharemarket for many years told me about a 'hot tip'. He said the product was about to take off and the word would get out any day now. He has a large portfolio and regularly has discussions with his stockbroker, so against my better judgment, I went ahead and bought some shares in his so-called 'hot-tip' company. I paid £500 for my small parcel of shares. Today, those same shares are valued at £14, a grim reminder that sits in my share portfolio in case I am ever in danger of forgetting that lesson.

ALWAYS REMEMBER THE GOLDEN RULE:
Never invest any money that you are not prepared to lose.

TIME TO TRADE

You have two options when it comes to buying and selling shares: doing it yourself online, or using a broker.

Online

This happens to be my preferred way of trading shares. There is a cost comparison to be found on www.aboutonlinetrading.co.uk and there are lots of online share-trading companies, including www.focus.squaregain.co.uk, www.etrade.co.uk and www.halifax.co.uk/sharedealing. Depending on which one you choose, you can expect to pay between around £1.50 and £15 for each 'trade', in other words each time you buy or sell shares.

Using a broker

A broker will cost you more than doing it yourself online. Even though I haven't been a big fan of brokers, plenty of my friends use them and have been extremely successful. The trick is to choose one with whom you get along and whom you trust. Use that great female instinct. You will be handing over thousands of pounds, so do your homework and start by asking friends or colleagues if they know someone they can recommend.

When you start talking to a broker make sure they understand your money personality type. Are you a risk-taker or do you want to be there for the long run and invest in shares that pay you a dividend? Once you have established a relationship with a broker you trust, you can then try to expand into the different sectors of the market, which is what Lillian did:

I had saved a few thousand pounds and I wanted it to earn better than the cash rate I'd get in a bank account. I'm not an expert in the sharemarket – I wouldn't know which share is doing better than another. I decided to contact a broker, through a free seminar that was advertised in the paper. The company had been around for some time so they were well established. I just didn't want to go to a broker I'd never heard of. The seminar was a chance to hear what they had to say.

I did have some money in a managed fund, and I owned property but I wanted to diversify my portfolio and buy some shares. I went along to the seminar and found the brokers to be very professional. The information was well delivered and easy to understand. They showed us some statistics that demonstrated they had been quite good in picking trends in the market. Having done some research, I could see that the stocks they were recommending did seem to be doing well. This gave me some confidence in their abilities and to be honest I don't have the time or the inclination to research every stock. So I decided to book an appointment and meet with one of the brokers.

I met Craig and we talked about my goals. I told him I didn't want high-risk shares. Based on what we discussed we made an agreement that he wouldn't contact me until he had a share that he felt I would be comfortable investing in.

I told him my goals were to invest in shares that were safe enough so that in two years or so, I could use this money to put a deposit down to buy a property. After our meeting I had to fill in a whole lot of paperwork and I remember thinking that the brokerage fee wasn't that much more than investing online. For my money, it was worth it.

I felt comfortable with Craig. I didn't feel as though he was going to rip me off or invest my money in something that I was uncomfortable with. The main thing I would say to anyone using a broker is to find someone with whom you're comfortable, someone who listens and who is not just using you to dump some shares. Don't be shy to speak up. If the first meeting doesn't feel right, just walk away. At the end of the day, you are paying them. Don't be intimidated by the Armani suits and plush offices. **Lillian, 34**

Lillian makes an interesting point about diversifying her portfolio. By this she means that she wanted to have exposure to various investment options. With any investment you will experience high and low periods. When you diversify your investments you have a better chance of backing a winner than if you had all of your eggs in one basket.

If you own property and have a managed fund then you have already diversified your investments. When property starts to boom you'll benefit by having a stake in the housing market. If property isn't doing so well you have the shares. It makes sense to have your money spread around to capitalise on the different areas of the market that do well at different times.

MANAGED FUNDS: TAKING OUT THE GUESSWORK

Managed funds are another type of investment, one that lets you invest in a range of things like shares and property without having to know anything much about them, and without having to have a lot of money. The best thing about managed funds is they take out all the guesswork. When you buy into a managed fund you are buying in with a whole lot of other people and there's a professional manager to run it.

Every day *The Financial Times* lists about two pages of managed funds and their performances. You should also visit www.morningstar.co.uk to compare and track how each fund performs via the percentage it returns across a period of one year, three years and five years. The star rating used alongside the funds is a great way of quickly seeing their performance. The Morningstar website also gives a list of other managed funds you can buy into.

As with any service provider, managed funds will charge you a fee for joining, and one for exiting. Usually you can expect to pay up to 5% of your invested amount as an entry fee (so around £250 if you're investing £5,000).

www.priceparadise.com offers a wide range of funds each with different (but low-priced) services. They have a number to choose from. They cover a range of different investment types, such as property, smaller companies, UK shares and international funds. You can diversify your risk by choosing to put money into a number of different managed funds. Having exposure across a number of funds will give you the opportunity to take advantage when each sector is booming.

Claire chose the online option when she wanted to buy into an investment fund:

Since I had a little spare cash sitting around after the sale of an investment property, I decided it was time to aim for a little more return than the 2.8% the bank was paying on a term deposit. The question was, which managed investment fund was going to earn good money, yet offer some security?

Being a regular newspaper reader, I began with the money section of my daily paper. I could see the UK economy was doing well. This was proven by many of my colleagues who like me were contractors and were picking up lots of new work. So I started looking for managed funds that invested in UK shares.

It was a bit of a no-brainer really. I just looked at the Morningstar website, considered the best performers and discounted any fund manager whom I hadn't heard of, then chose a couple of funds with good growth over a five-year period. No, I didn't choose the absolute top performer. To help the process, each fund has a star rating. I did no other research, made no phone calls to a financial advisor and did no more web trawling.

I made the investment through the Priceparadise website, which meant I paid very low entry fees. As a result of selecting funds investing in National Resources and in Asian equities (with J P Morgan and HSBC) the money has grown at well over 20% a year. Sure, this was a great result in a time of terrific growth of these sectors, but given I had chosen the best three-year performers, not the best one-year returns, I felt my chances of getting better longer term returns were greatly improved. **Claire, 36**

Claire makes it sound easy, but remember that before she bought into any fund she was familiar with investing and was aware of the booming economy. She is a regular reader of the finance pages, which helped her decision-making.

PROPERTY: AN INVESTMENT YOU CAN TOUCH

Thousands of Britons became millionaires in the recent property boom of the last five years. Quaint cottages and tiny units were suddenly worth a fortune if they were in the 'right' location. Everyone seemed to be caught up in it. Conversation at social gatherings was consumed by who was selling and who was buying. If you did not own property, you would have felt very left out indeed.

Recently the market has slowed down considerably, bringing out all the doomsayers. But now that the dust is beginning to settle, the property market is again looking better in the long term according to some.

The appeal of property is that it is tangible. With shares or managed funds, your money is put into a large pool with other investors. But when you invest in property you can see and touch what you have bought.

And once you've done your homework and bought property you'll have a great sense of achievement, just as savvy sisters Nell and Sharon have. Sharon explains:

My friends kept on telling me about the benefits to be had from doing a buy-to-let flat.

I began to think about it more seriously. I do own my car, but at the time that was all. Can you believe I was still living at home? So I didn't have a lot of expenses, and I knew that this was the best chance I would ever have to buy property. I was a little apprehensive about getting into debt, but I wanted to do it. I went back to the accountant and she explained things even further. I approached my younger sister, who was 27 at the time, to see if she was interested.

My sister Nell didn't own anything. I thought it would be good for us to do this together and share the load. If we got the right tenant, the costs would cover our loan repayment. Nell was really nervous and took a lot of convincing. I spoke to a friend who had done it recently and she was great. If someone you know has done it and you can ask for advice it really helps.

We ended up buying a new two-bedroom flat in the inner city. We looked at all the things like transport and the surroundings. There is a lovely park across the road and a new shopping centre with restaurants and cinemas not far away.

The place is rented out and we have had the same tenants in there for the whole four years we've had it. I'm really glad we did it and my accountant is particularly happy. **Sharon, 34**

This is what Nell had to say about investing in property:

Initially I was nervous of committing to an investment. I kept thinking about how I was going to keep up the payments – I didn't want to feel like I had to budget all the time and not go out.

I have a busy social life and I do earn enough to buy what I want. I love clothes and because I work for a large company I feel like I need to dress the part for work. But Sharon convinced me to go with her and look at some properties. I knew she would do it on her own if I didn't go in with her. Once we got started I really got excited about owning property.

We looked at a few two-bedroom flats and settled on a flat about two miles away from the city centre. We really loved the flat and we even considered moving in. But the idea was to get it for investment purposes.

I'm so glad my sister talked me into buying it. It is such an achievement. I felt really proud that I did it and I know that I have something to fall back on. It barely made a dent in my lifestyle, because we rented it out and the rent pays our mortgage. The flat itself has gone up in value; it was the best thing that I have ever done financially. **Nell, 31**

Before you set off to buy property, be clear about your objectives. For instance, if you are buying a small flat for the purpose of a buy-to-let scheme, as Sharon and Nell did, you must think like an investor and not be emotionally attached to the property.

Tax

All the expenses on the property (including maintenance and the interest you pay on your housing loan) can be deducted from the rental income you receive. Many people become interested in buying an investment property because they end up paying little or no mortgage costs after deductions and get all the increased value of the flat as profit when they sell.

If you sell an investment property for a profit, you will have to pay capital gains tax. The laws on this tax offset, and the tax you have to pay when you sell, have changed over time so it will depend on when you bought your property.

FEES AND TAXES

The purchase price of your property is only part of the story. On top of this you will have to fork out for many extras (these figures are only an estimate, but will give you an idea of what to expect).

Legal fees

If it's a fairly straightforward sale without too many delays or other issues, you can expect to pay around £400 – £750 for a legal professional, such as a solicitor.

Bank loan application fees

Fees will vary from lender to lender, but a loan application fee can cost around £500 if the loan is approved.

Stamp duty

You will need to allow for the stamp duty. This is charged on a sliding scale. Your loan provider or solicitor will give you an idea of what to expect. It is a percentage of the purchase price — if the price of your choice of flat or house is under a certain amount, currently £120,000, you don't have to pay it at all.

Agent's fees

This is usually a percentage of the purchase price, around 2.5% to 3%.

How much do I need for a deposit?

Most lenders prefer their customers to have at least 10% of the purchase price of the property to put down as a deposit before they approve the loan. But if you have a good relationship with your bank or lender they may approve your loan with a 5% deposit, provided you can prove that you have the money available and you have been genuinely saving for more than six months. The seller of the property will also have to believe in good faith that the remainder will be paid on completion of the sale. This happened a few years back when I sold an investment unit.

My husband and I had bought a small inner-city studio flat about five years beforehand and it was tiny but in a great part of town, close to transport, restaurants and cafes. In the five years we owned the place it had only lost two weeks of rental. Even so, we decided to sell. And even though the building had been renovated we knew there were some maintenance issues. After a few months, the real-estate agent said she had a buyer. He had put down 5% of the purchase price and was ready to sign the papers.

At first it seemed unusual to have only 5% but we thought if he had put the money down so readily then we were willing to sell. What also swayed us was that a month earlier we had another buyer who chickened out at the last minute. Not wanting to go through that again, we were happy to take the 5%. The rest of the sale went through without a problem.

Why extra payments on your mortgage make sense

Any financial planner will tell you that making payments fortnightly rather than monthly will cut years off your mortgage. Why? Because you are effectively paying off 26 repayments compared with 12. And if you make 52 weekly contributions instead of 48 (which is the monthly equivalent, i.e. 12 x 4), you'll chip away at your mortgage even faster.

Savvy savings tip

Some mortgage plans offer a redraw facility, which means you pay off your mortgage sooner but have money available if you need it. Lillian has found this very useful:

I have an investment property and it makes sense for me to put any extra money I have left over into my home loan account. It's reassuring to know I have money sitting there, plus it's eating away at my interest payments. Basically the more I can keep in there the more I can reduce my interest payments over the time of my mortgage. I'm way ahead of my payments now, and if I need the money for something like a holiday I can take that money back out of the loan account. **Lillian, 34**

Do your homework

Before you launch in and buy an investment property there are a few simple rules.

Know your market

If you have done some basic research, you will know what price you can expect to pay in any given area. To help you further you can look up recent sales in the area where you are interested in purchasing by visiting websites such as www.landreg.gov.uk and www.proviser.com. Also, visit the local real estate agents' websites, and if you want detailed lists of sales you can buy them at www.myhouseprice.com

Ask yourself, could I live here?

When assessing a property you intend to rent out it pays to consider whether you could live in the place yourself. Does it have facilities nearby such as cafes, restaurants and transport? Is it close to the major shopping centres? If you could happily live in the place there's a strong chance that someone else will want to live there.

Check your costs and maintenance fees

If you are thinking about buying an older house or flat, make sure you take into consideration any future maintenance and repair costs. It's true these costs are tax deductible, but you still have to have the money to pay for them upfront, and you don't want to overcapitalise on your purchase. This could happen if you get hit with a huge maintenance bill. When it comes to units, I particularly like smaller blocks because they generally have lower maintenance costs. Large blocks will have lifts, for instance, which are expensive to maintain, and big garden areas mean extra charges because they need ongoing maintenance.

Saving to buy together

Steve and Louise made an agreement that helped them save to buy their own home:

When I met my partner, Steve, he had been living with his uncle and saving really hard to get together a deposit on a flat, even taking extra weekend work just to build up this money. He then bought a small two-bedroom apartment in the suburbs. Around the same time my parents were downsizing from the family home and this meant I had to find somewhere else to live, so Steve and I decided to move in together.

The agreement between us was that Steve would make the mortgage repayments and I would save for our next property. We lived there for two years and in that time I kept my side of the bargain. When I was living with my parents I was spending my money on shoes, going out, alcohol, clothes ... life was one big party. But when I saw how hard Steve had worked to save that money, I wanted to try and save as well. I found it quite difficult at first, because I couldn't go to the hairdressers, or shop as often.

But I was motivated. The flat we were in was a little grotty and I wanted something nice – you know, inner city. Luckily, in the two years we had our flat it really appreciated in value. So we used the gains to buy the house we live in today.

The place we bought was the worst house in a good street. We didn't realise how much work it needed. To make the house livable we had to spend £9,000 on top of the purchase price. We made one major structural change, and that was to remove the wall between the lounge and dining room. This opened up the house and allowed the light to come through. We then had new floorboards put in, and painted the whole house ourselves.

In five years we'll be in a position to do more renovations, and in the meantime we both feel we've achieved something really good.

Louise, 29

Property for the single girl

I have just bought my second investment property. I don't need to have a man around. You know, a lot of my friends are not waiting for a man, they're just doing it themselves. **Kate, 26**

It goes without saying that sharing the expenses of buying a property is a huge benefit. Your expenses are halved and for many people it's an opportunity to own a place they couldn't have got on their own. But what about singletons? Trish explains why she decided to make the leap to buy a place on her own:

When I was 30 I decided it was time to buy my own home. My older brother and sister were married and had their own homes. I began to wonder if I would ever marry and settle down like they had.

I'm a solicitor for a well-known law firm. Even at the time I earned a good salary, around £45,000. But I had been renting for the previous five years and didn't have much to show for it.

It's not that I don't know where all my money goes. I only have to look in my wardrobe. I confess, I'm a shopaholic. You could say that shopping is my hobby. After a stressful week at work I love spending my Saturday mornings shopping. I've got expensive taste which means I tend to go for designer suits and shoes (they may be expensive but they do last longer!).

I was in a relationship that ended a year earlier and had found since the split that it was really hard meeting a guy that I liked, let alone imagine a future with. I was starting to worry and think to myself, I should have something to fall back on.

I started saving really hard and in six months I had enough for a deposit on an investment unit. With the help of my brother I began to look for places that I could buy. The only concern I had was that I was renting a gorgeous apartment in town and I didn't want to jeopardise that and downsize to something smaller to be able to meet the mortgage repayments. I needn't have worried.

I was prepared to spend between £175,000 and £200,000 on a flat. The bank agreed to lend me what I needed. The fact that I always paid off my credit card and had a good job helped.

Eventually I settled on a renovated two-bedroom apartment in a suburb close to the city. I liked it a lot and the block had eight flats, which meant low maintenance costs. I've had the flat now for four years and never had problems keeping it occupied. The rent virtually covers my mortgage. I feel very lucky to have bought it; thankfully the flat has appreciated in value. The whole thing has been a pain-free experience.

The other thing is that I don't feel guilty paying rent now, because at least I own a property. I've been able to claim back wear-and-tear, expenses and my interest on the loan. This helps reduce the amount of tax I pay even though I have a bigger income overall, which is another incentive because I do pay a lot of tax.

Today, the flat still looks great and one day, when I tire of city living, I'll move in there. **Trish, 34**

GETTING THE RIGHT FINANCIAL ADVICE
BEFORE YOU INVEST

Okay, so now you know about some of the basic investment categories and we've heard from women just like you who have taken the step into investing. If you're ready to do the same, where do you turn next? A financial advisor may be a good start. And don't worry if you think only wealthy people have financial advisors. A good financial advisor will want to be there from the beginning and help you to build your wealth, regardless if you have £10,000 or £100,000.

Finding the right financial advisor is rather like finding a good evening dress. You may have to try a few before you find one you're happy with. But rest assured good financial advisors are definitely out there. Seeking recommendations is definitely the best place to start. Ask family and friends, your accountant, your workmates and even the finance manager in your office to recommend someone.

If that doesn't turn up someone who sounds like they might be right for you, try the online directory of financial advisors at www.unbiased.co.uk. This site is designed to help you find a financial planner in your area. It includes some tips for choosing the best financial planner for you. The service is free to consumers and offers a listing of the licensed financial advisors around the country. You can search via postcode or product. The site also offers a free budget planner and financial feature articles.

Another useful contact that you should be aware of is the Society of Financial Planners at www.sofa.org. They can also provide details of financial planners in your area.

The first meeting you have with a financial planner should be free. In the meeting determine if the person understands your financial goals; where you are today and where you want to be. Once you find a financial advisor with whom you feel comfortable then they will charge a fee for the service they provide. This can be as a percentage of your overall portfolio (the money you want invested) or it can be on a commission basis. The main thing is for you to be clear on the fees and make sure there are no hidden charges.

Remember, this is your hard-earned money and you have a right to ask as many questions and to make sure the person you have chosen to be your financial advisor is working for you and not for themselves.

To check that the financial advisor you have chosen is licensed or for other legal checks on investment issues, contact the Financial Services Authority at www.fsa.gov.uk

COMPLAINTS AND WHERE TO GO

If something goes wrong and you find yourself in need of assistance there are organisations you can turn to. While they may not be able to solve your problems directly they will point you in the right direction. Try the Financial Complaints Commissioner (www.fscc.gov.uk)

on 020 7562 5530 or Financial Ombudsman Service (www.financial-ombudsman.org.uk) on 020 7964 1000.

The right investment for you will vary with your tolerance for risk. It will also vary depending on the stage of life you're at. Whenever possible you should have a piece of the action in several forms of investment. That way you protect yourself against losses as far as possible and increase your chance of profit. But no matter which form of investment you choose, the key to success is confidence and knowledge. And the good news is you can build both.

£130

CHAPTER TEN

KEEPING UP WITH THE HILTONS

You've got your credit card debt under control. You are making lots of small, painless savings and you have extra money which you are now investing. Okay, you are free to shop! Of course, we are talking about savvy shopping.

You can look like a million pounds without being an heiress. You can even have similar shopping fun to the Hilton sisters without the crippling bills (or, dare I say it, the loss of brain cells). Follow these simple rules and you'll discover that it's not hard at all.

TEN SIMPLE BUT SAVVY SHOPPING RULES
I. Set yourself an annual clothes allowance
In the first chapter we looked at ways you can cut back on

some spending so you can use this money for whatever turns you on. If your goal was to find more money for clothes or shoes, that's great, but set yourself a limit. A savvy girl knows she has planned for her annual allowance and can spend this how and when she likes, with no nasty surprises when the bills come in.

2. Remove the clutter

Do you have a wardrobe full of clothes but nothing to wear? Before you go out and buy another item of clothing, go through your closet and check to see what might be lying neglected at the back. The trouble with too many clothes is you'll forget what you have amid the clutter. It's frustrating to re-discover a useful work skirt just after you've bought another.

Feng shui followers talk about the benefits of de-cluttering their homes. Once you get rid of the clutter you bring new energy into your environment. The same rule applies for clothes: once you get rid of the old you make way for the new. So to bring some new items into your wardrobe you will need to get rid of any items you have not worn for, let's say, a year. Forget 'I may need it one day'. The reality is you will probably never wear it again. So, give it away or throw it out — or try selling it online.

3. Are you a trigger-happy shopper?

This scenario is one many of us can relate to. You've had a hard day at the office or you've had a run-in with someone. To help release some of your frustrations you decide to hit the shops. It's understandable – we all get pleasure from buying new things. But when you shop in an emotional state whatever you purchase will prove costly.

The last thing you want is to spend money on clothes you're not going to wear. If you are a trigger-happy shopper the main thing is to be aware of your state of mind. Instead of shopping when you feel stressed, call a friend or just go for a walk – in the opposite direction to the shops. Or just sit in a cafe and read a magazine.

Become a savvy happy shopper rather than a trigger-happy one.

4. Take a friend, not a group

It's great to go shopping with a trusted girlfriend. A true friend will tell it like it is. If the item is not flattering, you need someone who'll tell you straight.

But shopping with a group is not a good idea. It not only slows you down, because everyone has their own shopping agenda, you'll also be bombarded with a whole lot of conflicting opinions. You know they mean well, but in the end so many mixed messages will probably lead you to buying unwisely. Leave the group girlfriend experience for the nightclubs.

5. Buy quality not quantity

Savvy girls believe in buying one or two quality pieces at the start of each season. Yes, it's tempting to pick up something new every week but it's not money savvy, and if you're buying on impulse it's probably not fashion savvy either.

I know a woman who buys a piece of clothing, usually from the cheaper chains, wears it once and then throws it out. She does it so that she feels she always has the latest look. She believes the clothes aren't even worth washing, because 'they are so cheap they would probably fall apart after one wash. And they'll be out of season in a few weeks.'

It's easy to see she has more money than sense. But if you're buying a new skirt every second week and wearing each one just for a couple of months, you're not really so different to my wasteful acquaintance. Find out what really suits you, buy for quality and save money (not to mention cutting down on waste).

6. Soldes!

When I was 21 I travelled to Paris. As I wandered through the city centre I noticed a sign on a shop window: Soldes. At first I thought it was the name of the store, then shop after designer shop the sign appeared. I realised that I was in the midst of an end-of-season sale. Here I was in the capital of fashion and a sale was on! They had genuine bargains and I bought clothes that still look great today.

If you like designer clothes then train yourself to wait

for the sales. I swear the sale seasons begin earlier and earlier each year. To keep track of when they start, get onto the mailing lists of the fashion houses. Every well-known designer store has a database of loyal clientele and they will keep you informed of upcoming sales and often give you a chance to shop before the general public.

7. Avoid the lunchtime shopping rush

The ideal time to shop is in the early part of the day when there aren't as many shoppers out. I know that it often feels as though the only time you have available to get out there and shop is during lunch hour. But if you give in to that feeling you'll be madly competing with other rushed shoppers, you'll get little help from shop staff, who are at their busiest, and you'll be feeling hassled and possibly hungry – far from an ideal decision-making state. If you make yourself wait till a better time then you'll be more relaxed, you'll make better shopping choices and in the end you will save money. Can such a simple change really affect your monthly bottom-line? Absolutely!

8. Buy to fit your real body – not your dream body

This is tough for any woman. But it's time to come clean about your body image. We've all witnessed plus-size women squeezing into tight, ill-fitting clothes. Kim from the hit comedy 'Kath & Kim' is a perfect example. She thinks she's a babe but that spare tyre says otherwise.

Whether you are thin, plump, tall or small, choose the clothes that complement your body. You will get so much more wear out of them than you will buying an ill-fitting piece in the hope you'll fit into it 'one day'. Also, if you are buying clothes just to follow fashion and the look is not flattering for you, you're only wasting your hard-earned money.

9. If in doubt, leave it out

You have just tried on a pair of new shoes. You kind of like them, but you're not quite sure. The savvy thing to do is wait 24 hours, or at least till the end of your shopping expedition, then come back. If you still really want them then, buy them. But if you come back and you are still unsure, either bring a friend along for a second opinion or don't buy. And yes, they might be sold in the meantime. That's a risk worth taking. There will always be another pair around the corner. Reminding yourself of this when you're tempted but unsure is a tactic that could save you heaps. It's so simple, but so true: If you really need it you'll have no qualms about your purchase. If you hesitate, trust your instinct and leave it.

10. Shopping online

Savvy girls love a bargain and what better way to find one than to shop online? No need to fight for the attention of the salesperson here, you can shop in your time and find real savings. (By cutting out sales staff and the expense of running a boutique, the overall cost is usually much lower.)

Sure, there is a risk in buying sight unseen, although if you know the label and you happen to own clothes from this designer in your size, then you should be okay.

INTERNET SHOPPING

Buy and trade on eBay

With 21 million hits a month, this person-to-person auction website (www.ebay.com or www.ebay.co.uk) is probably the most popular trading venue on this planet. There is a saying that everything has a price. You name it and it will probably be on this site up for sale, from the expected to the unexpected. One guy even auctioned off his virginity!

Some savvy young women have sourced designer clothes and are selling them here much cheaper than the boutiques. It's really worth a visit. You do need to be cautious about payment. But it's worth noting that if you pay via a credit card through the 'PayPal' payment process, owned by the same company as eBay, you get buyer protection up to £500 of the purchase price.

Cosmetics

You can save quite a bit buying these items online, and there's no problem with sizing or colour choice! Here are some sites I've found useful:

- www.perfume.co.uk This sells genuine designer brand perfumes and cosmetics for men and women. The products on offer are remarkably reduced, some as much as 70% off the retail price. Watch out for regular internet specials.

Also worth a look:

- www.handbag.co.uk
- www.perfume-elite.co.uk
- www.strawberrynet.co.uk

Pharmaceuticals

You can get good savings on pharmaceuticals, vitamins and health needs at:

- www.oliphaunt.com
- www.compareonlinebeauty.co.uk
- www.thexton.co.uk

(Don't be tempted by overseas pharmaceutical sites. You don't have any consumer protection if the goods are fake, and if the item is not licensed for UK use it'll be stopped by Customs and you'll have blown your money.)

OTHER PLACES TO GRAB A BARGAIN

Now that you have these simple rules under your money belt, let's see where else you can find a bargain.

Haircuts

Some of the major hairdressing chains are always looking for models. Some of the major hairdressing salons have associated hairdressing academies and offer cheap haircuts, styles and colours to customers. Once you've found somewhere near you that operates like this you'll need to tell them what sort of thing you're after. One of their trained apprentices will usually cut your hair under the supervision of a senior hairstylist educator.

Magazines

Can't live without your weekly magazine fix? Save by subscribing instead of buying them at the newsagent. Check out the savings to be had by phoning the number of the magazine itself.

Second-hand/Nearly new shops for vintage finds

One girl's trash is another's vintage treasure. It's definitely worth visiting the best of the nearly-new shops and secondhand designer label shops — you never know what you might find. A friend of mine who always looks fantastic is only too proud to rattle off the details of her latest find, like a Stella McCartney jacket for £15.

Asda, Primark and Sharon Stone

For basics, aim to pay a basic price. If you find a good-looking white T-shirt at Asda ('George') or Primark, stock up and save a heap.

A few years ago, US actress Sharon Stone caused a stir as she walked down the red carpet at the Oscars. The paparazzi asked who had designed her outfit, which included an elegant, body hugging, basic black T-shirt. She stunned them with the news that she'd bought it at the inexpensive US chain The Gap. Sharon, your basic instinct proved a winner.

Factory outlet tours

Factory outlets have become increasingly popular. I can recall visiting US factory outlets about 10 years ago and wishing we had them here. Today they are in all capital cities and many large regional centres. They have become so popular that you can take special bus tours. You'll have to pay a fee for being driven around. But if you make a day of it with a couple of your girlfriends it can be a lot of fun. Just try not to fall for the trap of buying every bargain you see. A bargain is only a bargain if you needed that item in the first place.

There are too many bus tour operators to list, but log onto the web and search for factory outlet bus tours to see what's on offer in your area.

Discount shopping guides

A small booklet called 'Keep One Suitcase Empty: The Bargain Shoppers Guide to the Best Factory Outlets in England, Ireland, Scotland and Wales' gives a huge list of where to shop at wholesale prices. For the latest information just type 'factory outlets' in your internet search engine and see what takes your fancy!

CHAPTER ELEVEN

CHAT ROOM

No matter how far you are along the road from financially out of control to money savvy, you're not alone. The questions and concerns you have are ones other young women share:

RELATIONSHIPS

Maggie, 34, is starting to feel time is passing her by. She is keen to buy property but her partner has other priorities. Should she go it alone?

How long have you been together?
Two years.

Is this the real thing?

Yes, we're in a committed relationship. My partner is divorced and has two children. We rent a three-bedroom house and we share the rent, which is £275 a week. The house is larger than I would have liked, but we need it because every second weekend we have to have space for his children.

Do you want to buy property?

Yes, I turned 34 recently and I have started to think about us getting property. I've tried to broach the subject with my partner, but he really shies away from it. I want to talk about our goals but each time we try the conversation is strained. He is under pressure as he has to provide for his ex-wife and kids and I think he feels guilty that he has to put most of his money there and not into our relationship. I can understand that.

Do you have any savings?

I've saved £3,500 and I pay off my credit card each month. Luckily, I'm in a good job and I feel stable there, that's why I'd like to buy property now. But my partner is feeling the strain of having to provide for his kids. I don't want this to hold me back … but am I just being greedy?

Sometimes I get annoyed because he goes out, stays out late and then the next morning he complains about how much money he has spent. So I think, 'Alright then, I'll go on a revenge spend'. I seem to be doing that a lot lately.

What have you bought?
I've bought a dog and I really spoil her. I bought her a new doggy house, expensive shampoo, a doggy bed and all the knick-knacks. I've stopped now but I guess I did go overboard for a while. Maybe by spoiling her I felt rewarded in some way.

You know you could still buy property on your own or even better, you could buy something with a family member or friend.
I've been thinking about this a lot lately.

How will your partner react if you go it alone?
I think he would be really supportive, because if we do end up together forever at least I've made a start and he can come in when he feels less money pressure. I'm going to talk to him about this. I know my parents would help out. They'd be happy to go halves, as they are keen for me to have a place of my own.

Feedback
Maggie feels she is in a position to buy property and the timing is right for her. Her job is stable and her parents are there to help her. Maggie is doing the right thing in

THE SAVVY GIRL'S MONEY BOOK

seizing the opportunity to buy a place, even though her partner is not ready. It's hard to predict the future and what if they should separate? If that happens, at least Maggie would know she has something to fall back on. If they stay together then she has made a start for the both of them.

If you feel as though you are ready to take the plunge, like Maggie, don't let others hold you back. If this is something you want to do, find a way.

SINGLE IN THE CITY
Janette is a 25-year-old career working girl. Where does her money go?

Typically what do you spend your money on each day?
When I'm organised I try to buy a weekly bus ticket, since it saves on buying a ticket every day. If I pay as I go, it's really expensive. Another thing I spend money on is buying lunch. I really need to get organised. When I do the shopping on the weekend and have food in the house so I can take my lunch to work, then I'm happy with myself. But too often I just get lazy and then it really adds up — a drink and lunch can be as much as £5 to £7 a day, that's £35 week! It really annoys me because it is needless. I do spend a lot of money through the week. I'm really bad at having cash in my wallet. Sometimes I get only £20 out just so I don't have much in my wallet, then I find I'm doing

this often and to make it worse, the ATM withdrawal fees add up. From now on I'm trying to make the £20 last.

Do you have savings?

Yes, I've finally started doing it and now on my payday, I have 10% put straight into my savings account. I got organised enough to do it because I was paying so much rent. I hated handing over £590 to the landlord every time. It's a big wad of cash. I decided one day I would like to be on the receiving end.

At first when I started the savings account I would put money in, then find myself broke and take it out again. I had a conversation with my dad and he said, 'You have to be strict about it.' So I decided to have the money taken out automatically and put into a Lloyds savings account. After three months I have saved around £750.

I recently increased the amount being put into that account by 10% because I want to go to Morocco for two weeks. I plan to go in three months' time and I'm putting away £300 a month. It's really not that much and I don't miss it because it's being taken out automatically and I'm not aware of it. I'm living on whatever I have left and then I get to go on holidays!

Do you have credit cards?

No, I don't, but I have a multi-access card with debit card access. Too many of my friends have credit card debt. If I don't have the money then I shouldn't be buying, I think. If I don't have a card I don't use one.

What is your biggest weakness?
That's easy, spontaneous shopping. If I walk past something I like I'll pop in and get it. I don't really go shopping very often. But if I see something on sale I will be tempted to go in. The other day, I saw a swimsuit sale at Next. They had all these really nice bikinis and I couldn't go past when I saw they were only £25!

Going out is also a big drain on the wallet. I go out with my friends and we go drinking and clubbing. A couple of drinks at a bar and then it's off to a club and then it turns into a huge evening. I do have a tendency to have large evenings out with people. Sometimes I can spend £60 to £70 in one night. It really depends. If you make a decision about kicking on when you're not sober you end up spending way more.

I get paid monthly: the first two weekends of a pay period is great but by the third and fourth I'm usually restricted to video nights in.

Are you interested in investing?
I am. I do have this idea that I would like to gradually build wealth and have an investment property. I would like to buy property with someone I can trust. I haven't met the man of my dreams yet. At the moment I couldn't

afford it on my own. Who knows, maybe I'll do it in five years or so. I'm only 25.

Feedback

Janette is enjoying life and partying with her friends. Sure, she spends a lot when she goes out and she doesn't hold back on buying something she wants, like the swimsuit, even if she doesn't really need it. But at least she is aware of areas where she can cut back, like getting organised and making her lunch. She also has the right idea in relation to credit cards. If she doesn't have the money then she doesn't spend it. Taking her father's advice was good and now she knows that putting money aside is really not that hard. And that automatic savings arrangement will come in very handy when she does want to invest.

SAVING FOR A TRIP OVERSEAS

Maria, 24, and her boyfriend, Paul, 26, are working towards an overseas trip.

On a typical working day, what do you buy with your money, Maria?
I buy a weekly travel pass for £17.50 and keep £15 cash in my purse for coffee and snacks to last me the week. I know it's not much, but Paul and I are focused on saving for our trip.

Do you know how much you spend each day?
I know what I spend on a weekly basis. I budget a set amount each week for different things. So some weekdays I spend only £1.75 for the day, buying coffee. I usually buy my lunch once a week and occasionally buy snacks. If I go out for a meal on a weeknight my rule is that I have less to spend on entertainment on the weekend.

Do you have savings?
Yes, I have a set amount that goes into my HBOS account automatically each payday so I don't miss it. The money is for our trip.

Do you have credit card debt and if so do you pay your credit card off each month? How much, roughly, would you carry on your card a month?
I have a credit card with a small limit. I try to pay it off straight away and avoid paying interest. The longest I've let it carry over is three months; that was a couple of hundred pounds. I use a direct debit Visa card for groceries and other predictable costs.

That's great. So you have very little debt?
Yes, I prefer it that way.

Are you renting, and if so, how much do you pay?
Paul and I rent a two-bedroom apartment. I pay £95 a

week and he pays £145 because he uses the second
bedroom as an office.

What is your biggest spending weakness?
I'd say last-minute shopping for clothes and shoes. I am
indecisive and put off buying outfits until the day before
a special occasion. I end up spending more than I expect
to, out of desperation!

**Are you interested in buying investment property or
that sort of thing later on?**
This is definitely on the cards, but not for a couple of
years — right now travel is our first priority. If we buy in
the inner city then we won't be able to afford to do much
except pay off the mortgage.

Feedback
Maria is a perfect example of someone who follows just a
few simple rules for great results. First up, she only has a
small amount of cash in her wallet each week, cutting out
temptation. She takes lunch from home most days and will
occasionally treat herself to a snack plus one bought lunch
a week. She even has a debit card, so when she spends using
the card to buy goods, the money is taken directly out of
her bank account. This means she is spending the money
that she has, rather than 'maxing out' her credit card. If
Maria's habits are anything to go by then she will have no

problems saving for a house or any other investment in the future. Have a great trip, Maria.

SOLO SINGLE ADVENTURER

Fiona, 26, is also saving for a trip—a solo jaunt to the USA.

What's your saving method?

I have £50 taken out of my salary each week and put automatically into an Abbey National savings account. I've saved around £750 in the last three months.

I have travelled before and also saved for my last holiday this way. I do find some weeks I'm really low on cash but I really want to go overseas, perhaps even live in Europe for a while, so I have strong motivation.

I spend a lot of my money on going out. I live near the city and I like to go to the local pubs and clubs with my girlfriends for drinks and dinner. I don't own a car and I rent a flat, so I own nothing of significance.

Luckily, I don't buy magazines, nor do I smoke and I bring my lunch every day. The money I have left is for going out with my friends.

Do you think because you want to travel it's easy to cut back on other things?

Yes, it's pretty easy. I was earning a lot less, working as a waitress, when I travelled the first time and I managed it then. I earn more now as a graphic designer. I don't spend much on clothes because I like to buy individual things that I can pick up from markets and second-hand. Most times they're really cheap. I do love a bargain.

I don't feel the urgency to buy things because I'm going overseas.

What about the future, once you've finished travelling?
I'm only 26 and I really find it hard to look into the future. When I look at the price of property today I wonder if I'll ever be able to afford it. My older sister and her boyfriend recently bought a property and it's miles away from the city, way out in the suburbs. I feel that's the sacrifice you have to make if you want to buy a house. I've just moved into the city having come from the country and don't want to live way out there any more ... well, for a while anyway.

Would you consider buying a property as an investment? That way it doesn't matter where it is, as long as it's good for rental returns and you could live where you like, knowing you've got a foot in the market. Oh definitely, that's really a good idea. A friend of mine is my age and she has done exactly that, all on her own!

Does this mean you and your girlfriends have decided not to wait for a guy to come along before you buy property? Do you think you may end up on your own?

Yes, I do. I've just recently started a relationship and in the back of my mind, I think we're the 'Sex and the City' generation. We might end up being single, and I know some of my friends are happy and fine with this. I think we know that we don't need someone to help us get by in life, or buy a house. If I reach the age of 35 and am single, I would definitely buy a place.

Some of my friends are just doing it now, buying property and not waiting for the traditional 'boy-meets-girl-and-they-buy-a-house-together' scene. But I'd still like to think that I will meet someone and we'll buy a place together.

Feedback

Fiona will have no problems saving for a property, having already saved for an overseas trip. Most people who have saved in the past, whether it is for a trip, wedding or car, have no problems when they want to commit to saving for something even bigger. It takes the same discipline, it's just the amount of money that's different.

BUYING PROPERTY SOLO

Andrea, 28, is an engineer working for a large government department. She already owns two properties. How did she do it?

Andrea, are you paying rent where you live? Where does most of your income go?
Yes I'm renting; I pay £140 a week. I own two investment

properties and most of my money goes towards the mortgages I have on both.

Do you feel you are sacrificing a lot to keep up the two mortgages? Do you still go out and have fun?
I don't feel I make sacrifices at all. I've been fortunate that the properties I've bought give me great returns and they virtually pay for themselves. I'm not out of pocket by much.

What got you started? It's fairly unusual for someone so young to have achieved this.
I guess I've always been a person who lives within their means and I earn more than I spend. By the time I was 23, which is when I bought my first property, I had actually saved up quite a bit of money. I didn't have the money earmarked for anything else and my parents suggested that rather than having it sit in a high-interest savings account, I should invest in property, which is more solid. That's really how I got started. Then two years later I used some inheritance money as part of the deposit to buy the second one.

Where are your properties?
One is in the city and the other is just on the outskirts of the city. I've never had any issues with renting them out.

So you have always been a saver; why aren't you into other things like clothes and make-up?

I've been working since I was 16 and I have always earned enough for my needs. It's not that I'm deliberately a saver, it's just that I'm not that extravagant. I've always had a bit left over and that's what I saved. It wasn't a deliberate plan.

Is your whole family like you?
No, my younger brother is constantly in debt. He's always borrowing money from me.

As a 23-year-old was it easy to get a home loan from a bank?
I found the bank was very suspicious of me. I think they saw this young, single female and wondered how on earth I could have that sort of money saved up. They kept saying things like, 'Did you save up all this money yourself?', 'Is this really all your own money?'

Are you in a relationship?
No, I'm single and I think this was another issue for the bank. They probably would have preferred lending to a couple. I think they see couples as more financially secure and likely to be in it for the long term.

What sort of research did you do before you bought your properties?
First, when I'm in the process of buying, I go and look at quite a lot of apartments. I get a feel for the prices of

properties in the area. I'll look at 15 to 20 properties before I buy. I know the inner-city suburbs, so I have a good feel for what the rental market will pay. Also, when I bought my second property it was already being rented. So it was good to know that the property I bought already had someone in it. I didn't have to worry about whether I would find a tenant.

I also look at the rental return. Basically I'm looking for anything greater than 5% growth each year.

What would you say to someone who is just starting out with a savings plan?
I have always said that it doesn't matter whether you save £5, £50 or £500, but you have to save something every week. You can start small. It is always worth having money on the side so you can do what you want to do when the right time comes.

Apart from buying properties, what else do you enjoy?
I travel every year. This is a very important part of my lifestyle. I try to find somewhere new each time and usually take a month off. I don't stay in expensive places, I'm happy to stay in hostels. It's more about the experience, not the accommodation you're in while you're there.

What places have you travelled to?
America, Europe, Mexico, Thailand. My next trip is to

Australia and New Zealand. I have some friends there who are doing the working-holiday thing.

To travel each year and own two properties you must earn a good wage?
I do, it's around £48,000.

Feedback
As you can see, I had quite a lot of questions for Andrea. For someone so young she has an impressive record. It's true that she earns a good salary but she is doing the smart thing and making her money work for her while she is young and has the capacity to earn a good wage. It's also true that she inherited a bit of money, but don't forget she'd already saved for one deposit on her own before this. She makes sure she enjoys her life and doesn't feel as though she compromises on anything. Andrea is one savvy cookie!

TIME FOR A CAREER CHANGE

At 33, Samantha is uncertain whether she wants to continue working as an accountant. Some fatherly advice seems to have hit home.

How important is your job?
I've been working as an accountant for more than 10 years and for the past year, I have been looking for a change. I now realise I don't want to be an accountant for the rest of

my life. The everyday processes have become so mundane and boring. And I used to work long hours — weekends and late nights. But my boss never appreciated or commented on the long hours I put in. In fact, he started clock-watching and if I was 10 minutes late he would pull me up on it. Now work is no longer a priority.

I'm really not sure what I want to do and this is frustrating me, I'd really like to have a total career change and try something creative. I'm starting to think more about the future. I used to think I don't care about owning my home. I thought I'd meet the right guy and we'd work towards this together. Now that I'm 33 I can't rely on that. My parents are on at me to buy a place and stop renting. I don't want to get to 40 and still be renting, or worse still be renting at 60 and have these sorts of worries.

What do you spend your money on?
I love clothes, jewellery and going out. In the past I used to go out every night, Monday to Friday. I still never cook for myself. I rent an apartment in a nice part of town (close to the city and I can walk to work). Most of my salary goes towards these things. I have to say, after I went to Asia last year and saw how cheap the clothes were I am more cautious about how much I spend on clothes.

Do you have any debt?
I have no debt whatsoever, not even a credit card. I know

this is hard to believe. I grew up in a family where my father paid cash for everything and he hated being in debt. He has influenced me to use cash. I do have a debit card. I realised I needed some access to cash, particularly as I travel every year. I can at least take the cash out when I'm in another country with my debit card. The money is waiting in my bank account. I just prefer to do it that way.

I must be the only young, single, city girl without a credit card. My friends can't believe it. I do have an account with money I have put away in a term deposit. I don't touch this. I own nothing and I guess it does concern me, but I do have my parents to fall back on. If I need anything, I go to my parents. My father taught me the importance of education. Today he says to me, 'Don't rely on a man, because there are no guarantees that he will be around forever.' My father believes I need to look after myself.

One day I would like to think I could meet someone and get married and have kids. I know I will never give up work, unlike my mother. I love the fact that I can travel every year. It's my money. I have been thinking I would like to buy a house. It's getting older that has got me thinking that way, and as my dad says, there are no guarantees even if you have a man in your life.

Feedback

At first glance Samantha's life looks rosy, with no debts and an annual overseas holiday. And she has a great social life to boot. But there are some problems here.

The number one issue for Samantha is her unhappiness in her job. This may be a good time for her to speak with a career counsellor, someone who can guide her to work out what she wants to do.

It's true that Samantha does have money and could possibly buy an investment property, but she needs to decide what she's going to do in her working life first. If she has to re-train in order to change her whole career path this will mean time off work and therefore no income. Samantha will need to spend some time to find the direction she wants to take with her career before she considers any investments.

CHAPTER TWELVE

FIGHTING THE CINDERELLA CONSPIRACY

This book opened with one fairytale. Let's revisit another we all know well. It's the story of Cinderella, who slaved away every minute, dreaming of the day her Prince Charming would rescue her. Sure enough, her prince arrived and whisked her away to a world of castles and ladies-in-waiting; free from chores forever.

But it's time to let go of the fairytale once and for all. If you are pinning your hopes on being rescued from your job, you are making yourself a victim of the Cinderella conspiracy. You need to step out of your dream and wake up to the real world. I know this sounds a little harsh, but think about Gillian, who is approaching 50 and hasn't met Mr Right:

I have a great job in the corporate world and I earn good money. I can't believe that I'm almost 50 and I haven't met the right man. Sure, I've been out with a lot of men and even had some long-term relationships. I know we talk about meeting princes, but let me tell you, there are a hell of a lot of frogs to kiss first. Maybe I'm kidding myself, but I still hope to meet the man of my dreams.

I do spend a lot on my appearance and my friends say I look great for my age. I guess that's where most of my money goes – on clothes and beauty treatments. I have my hair done every week. The reality is that I'm now competing with younger and more attractive single girls.

I really believed that by now I would have been married with kids. I'm so tired of working hard and I have left it so late to start putting money away. I only started putting some money away about three years ago but luckily I now have enough for a deposit on a flat. Can you believe I've been renting for almost 30 years! If I had bought a small flat a few years earlier, I would have made a big dent on my mortgage by now.

My biggest fear is that the bank will not lend me the money because I'm getting older, even though my credit is good and I have always paid my credit cards on time. All I can say is thank God for my job. Luckily I started a pension payment plan which is piling up for when I retire.

I'm sure you know someone like Gillian who wonders how life has passed by so quickly and who hasn't found someone to settle down with. Gillian's saving grace is her job and the security it gives her. I wish Gillian the best, and it is great she has finally made a start. But I also wish she'd had a friend to give her some good financial advice 20 years ago.

WHY MARRIAGE IS NO LONGER THE ULTIMATE PLAN

Not so long ago young girls expected to meet their perfect match and settle down to married life and children. A job of their own, let alone a career, was rarely part of the picture. Now the focus is on education and careers. It's wonderful to be living in an age when women can be and do anything we choose.

Marriage is definitely on the cards for many young women, but often not until they are in their thirties. And as we know, the divorce statistics are very high. As well as getting married later, women are waiting longer till they have babies. It really is great to have a lot of options, but it means that you need to think about the fact that if you have a baby in your late 30s, you will still be supporting that child in your late 50s – all the more reason not to let your career go by the wayside.

Tania had a great job as a senior manager for a large telecommunications company but after the birth of her first child eight years ago she made a decision she now regrets:

When I was in my 20s I was self-assured, healthy and I had lots of energy. You know what they say, 'The world's your oyster.' When you are young you can indulge in everything: your friends, your job and your relationship. You have time to think and to develop what you want to do. And despite the impending birth of my first child, I thought things were not going to change too much.

Up until I had my son I thought all working mums over-dramatised their situation. I worked right up until a couple of days before he was born. I really enjoyed my job and planned to go back.

But while I was on maternity leave, I was looking casually at the job ads and I saw a job with more flexible working hours advertised. I thought this would allow me to leave the office earlier in the day, which seemed very attractive. I applied for it just to see what happened and I was offered the job. I made a hasty decision to take it, and this proved to be the biggest mistake. I am now in a job where I am just another faceless number.

I know we make choices in life and I made a conscious decision to give myself to my family (we now have two kids). I have fulfilled the family role but not my work role, which is a shame.

We have a mortgage and I need to keep working. We have an army of friends and family who help with the kids. I'm so lucky in that respect. My husband also changed his job to take on a role within a government department. This means he can finish earlier and pick up the children from school on some days, the other days a friend drops the kids home.

Now that I'm a working mother, I have renewed respect for other working mums. I sometimes think there is too much pressure to achieve it all. There is so much information overload, that we get distracted from what we really want out of life. I now know I would have been happier in my old job, where they treated me with respect. I went from running a department to a much lesser role. Today, my job just pays the bills. **Tania, 37**

Tania's story makes it clear that even when you have a family you love, work is still important. She misses the challenges in her previous job, and perhaps regrets not trying to get more flexibility in a job she was happy with. For other mothers, being at home full-time right through their kids' pre-school years is their preferred option. It's only when you're in the position of making that decision that you'll know what's really right for you. But when it comes to making arrangements that suit you and your family, your job is definitely part of the mix. As pioneering photo-journalist Margaret Bourke-White put it, 'Work is something you can count on, a trusted life-long friend who never deserts you.'

MORE CHOICES, MORE CHALLENGES

Your parents' generation was likely to have worked in nine-to-five jobs and stayed in the same jobs for many years, in fact, often as long as 40 years, which is unheard of today. Perhaps they even earned long-service leave, a term you may not have ever heard, let alone seen in action.

With full-time and long-term employment becoming a rarity, your working life will be very different to theirs. A little more than 40% of jobs are now casual or contract, and this is on the increase. Today's working environment means that your career is likely to be a jigsaw put together from the following pieces:

FREELANCE WORK

- Contract work
- Casual and part-time work, including job sharing
- Project work — working for an assigned period on one specific task
- Shift work — particularly in fast-growing service industries such as hospitality
- Working from home

That's fine — it suits many of us, like these career girls:

I really enjoy meeting new people and everyday there's something unexpected and different. **Isla, 29, national account manager**

I find it incredibly satisfying to identify and analyse problems with our current business operations and then successfully implement solutions to these problems. **Tina, 35, information technology business analyst**

I work on interesting projects. I'm constantly learning and no two days are ever the same. **Rachel, 33, help-desk manager**

I like all the options available to me as an accountant, there are so many different career paths, industries and locations that I can choose from. **Ann, 29, financial analyst**

But there are concerns, too. The three issues that stand out, no matter whether you are working in a traditional full-time job or in short-term contracting roles, are the following:

1. Long hours
2. Less security
3. Increased pressure in the workplace

If you're feeling consistently overworked and insecure, you are not alone.

Most people now in the early stages of their working lives will have 10 different jobs and three or four types of careers before they are finished, and the switches may not all be voluntary. Being money savvy means that your stress is kept to a minimum when those big changes occur.

Welcome to the world of actors and models

Actors and models have long been familiar with short-term work and the inevitable downtimes between jobs. Now the rest of us are finding out what it's like. Sharelle's brief working history is an example of one based around short-term assignments:

I'm only 24, but I have moved in and out of a number of jobs. I've done secretarial, restaurant work and worked in a sports shoe shop. I've been lucky enough to have work when I really needed it. I have my name down with a number of employment agencies. Sometimes I get anxious in between jobs, but I keep in regular touch with the agencies.

I really enjoy the freedom of working on a casual basis or temping. The down side is I don't have a long track record for being in one place long enough. The banks don't want to know you if you don't have a good working history. I may have a problem applying for a car loan, which I want to do, or even a credit card. Some of my friends envy me because they think my life is flexible. It's true, I can plan to take time away – there are benefits – and I also like the variety of people I meet. I must admit, I have developed into a good saver as well, I have to be, otherwise I can't meet my rent payments. **Sharelle, 24**

Sharelle is right to have concerns about the bank giving her a loan when she needs one, because she does change jobs regularly. A good track record of savings, and keeping up regular credit card payments will help.

ARE YOU REALLY IN THE RIGHT JOB?

Think of it this way, you will spend most of your adult life working. So it makes sense to take the time to find out what you really want to do. Have you chosen the right career?

If you are uncertain about your job, one way to help clarify your options is to speak with a career counsellor or career advisor. A career counsellor will look at areas in your life such as your lifestyle and your income and what your long-term goals are. Some organisations are bringing career counsellors on board and offering their services to their employees.

If you are working for a large organisation or government department, check to see if they have someone available – start with the Human Resources department. Of course you will need to be discreet, so that you are not seen to be looking around for a new job.

If your company doesn't offer this service, then phone your local council for free information on various careers. If you wish to enlist the services of a career counsellor or career coach, you can expect to pay anywhere from £100 to £300 per session (this gets cheaper if you book several!).

When IT manager Sarah became disillusioned with her job she decided to get some expert help. After a few sessions she is feeling a lot happier about her future:

I've been in the IT area for over eight years and to be honest I really feel as though I've had enough. When I started in the industry it was exciting as new developments in telecommunications evolved. But lately the industry has just gotten so tough, and it's hard coming in every day wondering if I'll get the axe.

I decided it was time to see a career coach. I got the name from a friend of mine who had some success from using one. When I made the appointment, Vanessa, the coach, asked me a whole lot of questions, like what my goals and aspirations were, and where I wanted to be and what I valued in my job. We also looked at what skills I have. She then devised a plan to help me meet some of the goals. My goals weren't financial, as I already owned my home and I had some other investments, like shares and funds. I had always earned good money and had some sense to put money away for a rainy day. I think I knew that I didn't want to be in IT all my life.

I'm a good manager and very well organised. What I came to realise was that I needed something that would allow me to express some creativity. Now I have my sights set on opening a small B&B in the West Country. A friend of mine who is also disillusioned with her job is keen to come in as a partner. I'm really excited about the prospects. I'm starting to feel energised again when I look to the future. I hope to achieve my dream within four years. **Sarah, 35**

Where to go

If you are uncertain about your career or future directions, there are several public and private services available to give advice. The starting point is usually free. Try www.jobcentreplus.gov.uk (it is not just for the unemployed – I promise!) or www.proteusconsulting.com (0870 760 6985) for starters.

This association is national, with members who provide advice for people seeking to enter the workforce or change their work direction. The website has a search facility for finding counsellors in your area.

Women's organisations and networking

Networking can be one of the most powerful assets you have in your working life. Just look around and you'll probably find you know someone who has landed a job through the connection of a friend, colleague or associate.

Elizabeth is a journalist whose last three assignments have come through contacts:

The work I do tends to be on a short-term or project basis. Over the last five years I've had three contract assignments. All these jobs came through industry contacts. I make sure I keep in touch with my friends and colleagues, not just because I'm after a job, but because we all look out for each other. The very nature of my job means I have to keep in touch with my associates, otherwise I could be out of a job for ages.

The other day a friend was looking for a job and she sent an email to a whole lot of contacts, saying she was available for work. She asked if we could forward her details onto anyone we knew who could use her services. Within two weeks she landed a job. **Elizabeth, 36**

There are dozens of women's networking groups across the UK. Search on the web for women's business networking organisations.

TIPS TO HELP YOU FIND A JOB

Here are a few tips to help you along the way:

- Search internet recruitment sites to see what's out there, how much it pays and what qualifications and experience you'll need. Start with:
  www.jobcentreplus.gov.uk
  www.proteusconsulting.com
  www.jobsearch.co.uk
  www.careerenergy.co.uk
- Daily newspapers – get into the habit of reading the careers sections.
- Read specialist magazines and websites that are

relevant to your industry or the one you want to break into.

- Network. Don't ever forget the power of friends and colleagues.
- Recruitment firms. Make an appointment with a recruitment agency that works within your field to get a feel for what is happening in the marketplace, and what sort of salary you can expect based on your experience. This service is free to you (the employer pays the agency costs).
- Update your CV. Have a friend or colleague go through it to make sure you haven't missed or downplayed anything that could be important. And make sure you're honest, don't invent things in hope of getting a job.
- When you're applying for a particular job, or if you get an interview, research the company in question. Check out their website and search other sources for news about them.

WORKING FROM HOME

Maybe you have decided to take the plunge and start your own business. No more clock-watchers hovering over you and pointless meetings. You're able to choose the hours you want to work and the portable office means you no longer have to be tied to your desk — cafés have become the second office for many people who work from home.

Setting up a home office can be quite expensive, but on the other hand, you can claim the costs of running your home office against your income. For example, if you are renting your home, part of the rent can be claimed as a business expense and so can relevant phone costs and a percentage of your utility bills. You should check with your accountant for details about what you can and can't claim.

Savvy girl Diana, 34, decided to go along and start her own business from home. Some clever thinking and assistance from her partner have helped cut down some of her set-up costs.

I have been a travel consultant for more than 10 years. When I turned 33, I decided I wanted to start my own business. I'm in a serious relationship and my partner and I have discussed having a child soon. But before that happens I wanted to make sure I was set up to work from home.

I had maintained a good relationship with my former employer. And with the help of my partner, I set up a computer system and software package that enables me to log into the network of that previous employer and use their resources. This proved to be a win-win situation for me and my ex-employer because I didn't have to buy the network software used by travel agents, which saved me a lot of money, and they get a percentage of the fee I earn when I book any travel.

Now with the business up and running, I feel that I can still keep earning income when the time comes for us to have a child. **Diana, 34**

Make your set-up work for you

It doesn't matter which road you decide to take when it comes to your career, whether you choose to be your own boss, freelance for other companies or be part of the corporate world, the important thing is that you are able to maintain an income. Use this valuable time, while you're working, to put money aside. Remember, your earning years should also be your saving years.

£250

CHAPTER THIRTEEN

THE LAST WORD

I hope this book, and the stories you've found in it, have inspired you to make some changes in your life. It doesn't matter how big or how small. Even if all you do is choose to open the 'no-touch' bank account or start to pay off your credit card debt regularly, you're on your way to being money savvy.

The important thing is to just start. Once you do there is a domino effect and other things start improving as well. Remember how Rhonda started out with nothing and then when she set her mind on the goals she wanted to reach, everything else fell into place?

Sure you'll encounter obstacles along the way. That's life. The women who've shared their stories can help you

THE SAVVY GIRL'S MONEY BOOK

see that even when things haven't been going so well, a few changes can turn everything around. And nothing beats the satisfaction you'll feel when you reach your goals.

Once you have gained some financial independence, be proud of it and help others. Don't forget, it's okay to talk about money. In fact you're crazy if you don't, whether you have it or not. We all learn from sharing our stories.

I also hope that you come away from this book knowing that what's important isn't really how much you earn, but what you do with it. Being rich is not just about your monetary worth. True richness comes from being able to enjoy your friends, family and work — in short, your life — as well as all the goodies that being money savvy will bring your way.

INDEX

ACKNOWLEDGMENTS

There are a number of people that I have to thank for helping me bring this book to life. First and foremost, my wonderful commissioning editor Hazel Flynn, I am so fortunate to have you be a part of this book. To my sisters, Leila, Rhonda, Noelle, Sonia and brother, Emile, there are no words to describe the support you have given me. This book wouldn't be complete without the inspirational voices of all the young women who shared their stories, thank you. To four friends who encouraged me along the way, Anne Archer, Dianne Hill, Josephine Brouard, Susanne Kirby. To the team at Murdoch Books, thank you for your enthusiasm and support. Finally, to my husband Glenn, for your ongoing support and to our sons Daniel and Marc, a big heartfelt thanks to all.

First published in 2005 by Pier 9, an imprint of Murdoch Books Pty Limited
This UK edition published in 2006 by Murdoch Books Pty Limited

Murdoch Books Pty Limited Australia
Pier 8/9, 23 Hickson Road, Millers Point NSW 2000
Phone: 61 (0) 2 8220 2000   Fax: 61 (0) 2 8220 2558

Murdoch Books UK Limited
Erico House, 6th Floor North, 93-99 Upper Richmond Road,
Putney, London SW15 2TG
Phone: 44 (0) 20 8785 5995   Fax: 44 (0) 20 8785 5985

Chief Executive: Juliet Rogers
Publisher: Kay Scarlett
Commissioning Editor: Hazel Flynn
Design concept and designer: Gayna Murphy
Editor: Siobhán Cantrill
Editor, UK adaptation: Kate Oldfield
Production: Monika Paratore

ISBN 1 74045 794 3
A catalogue record for this book is available from the British Library

Printed in China by Midas Printing (Asia) Ltd
Design and illustration copyright © Murdoch Books Pty Limited 2005
Text copyright © Emily Chantiri 2005